Appalachian Adventure

Jim Hill

Johanna and Bob,

Stopping at your house to rest and recharge was a treat.

Jim

ISBN: **1495489639**
ISBN-13: **978-1495489631**

Cover photos by Doug Hill
Cover Design by Karin Curtis-Hill

This book tells about my thru-hike of the Appalachian Trail to the best of my memory. A few of the names have been changed.

Contents

1 SPRINGER MOUNTAIN

In 1973, having returned from Vietnam and recently been discharged from the Army, I decided to hike the Shenandoah section of the Appalachian Trail before entering the workforce. It took me ten days to complete. Hiking in the beautiful Shenandoah Mountains of Virginia and breathing the fresh mountain air, I could feel my body and spirit re-charging with each passing day. Each night I would stay in a shelter and meet new people. Often we would sit around a campfire and have interesting conversations. I can remember things that happened during that hike like they happened yesterday.

One night I was awakened by something softly brushing my cheek. I automatically started to brush it away then realized I was face to face with a skunk. It started to arch its back. I froze and didn't move a muscle as we stared at each other for ten long seconds before it decided to move on.

I shared the shelter with a man who told me that during the night he had watched us sleeping from his astral spirit floating overhead.

My last night was spent with two enthusiastic thru-hikers. They were generous enough to share some of their adventures with me. It sounded fun. I remember thinking: "Someday I'm going to thru-hike the Appalachian Trail."

On April 28th 2009, three days after I retired on my 62nd birthday, I started hiking the Appalachian Trail. I picked Wingo as my trail name. Wingo was my loyal, happy, cocker spaniel and we spent many hours hiking together.

I had backpacked most of my life but never for more than three weeks at a time. Now I was going to be backpacking for months at a time. I didn't have a clue what such a long hike would be like, so for the past three years I had been reading hiker's journals on TrailJournal.com. It also had a forum where hikers would have their questions answered by experienced hikers. I learned a lot from Trail Journals. It helped me figure out the best way to hike my hike.

I didn't see this hike as a life changing event. I mainly wanted to have a good time. This looked like it might be fun. Now it was really happening. There were butterflies in my stomach. "Oh my Gosh! Here I Go!" It was almost dark when I started hiking. I hiked for a half mile and found a little spot about the size of my sleeping bag, five feet from a stream. Now it was dark. I decided to cowboy camp. This was the only time I cowboy camped the whole trip. Cowboy camping is when you sleep under the stars without a tent. I camped other times with just the netting of my tent, but this night was true cowboy camping. I got into my sleeping bag at 10:00 pm. It was chilly. My 20 degree sleeping bag felt good. It was a calm, night. The water made little soothing tones as it splashed in the stream. I relaxed, took a few deep breaths, gazed at the stars, and wondered what my future held.

I wish I could say I slept soundly. I didn't. I heard sounds in the night - twigs snapping, noises I couldn't identify. Something quickly scampered over me and woke me up. My heart was pounding.

I woke with the dawn, had a couple of Pop Tarts, packed up and continued to the top of Springer Mountain which was the official starting point of the Appalachian Trail. When I reached the top I was greeted by Many Sleeps. He was a ridge runner with a long, completely white beard. Ridge runners are like forest rangers but spend more time on mountain trails. For many years he had signed hikers in at the Trail register and started them on their journeys. He had been mentioned in hiker's journals over the years and it was fun to actually meet him in person. He was a gracious man.

I started my hike through green, healthy forest. Once in a while I do something right. This was one of those times. I stopped at 2:00 pm. I had hiked nine miles but it was only 2:00 pm. I had six more hours of daylight that I could hike. I didn't. I put my tent under fragrant pines swaying in the breeze. I sat down on a fallen log, relaxed, and audibly groaned! I could feel every muscle in my body.

I very slowly went about camp chores: Filling water bottles from the stream, getting the interior of the tent organized to sleep in, taking a sponge bath, changing into my camp clothes, and washing my hiking clothes. I bought some special soap to do this – Dr. Bonner's Magic Soap. It advertised that you could wash your body, hair, and clothes with it. For a wash basin I had a five liter portable container that weighed ounces and folded up to the size of my fist. One of my pre-hike goals was to not smell like a hiker. I was going to have a sponge bath and wash my dirty clothes each day after hiking. (I can hear you chuckling!) It didn't happen. My goal lasted about three days. It was hard putting the cold, wet clothes on in the morning. The soap had a strong pleasant peppermint smell that I worried would attract bears as my clothes dried in the tent overnight. I realized early on that being clean and smelling good was a battle I wasn't going to win, so I stopped worrying about it. When my smell got too bad, I would take a sponge bath and wash my clothes with the Dr. Bonner's soap. It didn't happen all that often. I still have about ¼ of the original 4 ounce bottle of Dr. Bonner's soap.

After dinner I hung the bear bag on a high branch and went to bed at 8:00 pm. I was very tired and slept like a baby. I awoke to the sounds of birds singing in the trees. It was a beautiful morning. My legs, back, shoulder, arms, neck, feet.... hmmm.... Let's try this another way: What wasn't sore?.......My right eyebrow.

I was eager to start the day. It was slightly chilly at first but there were lots of climbs and I warmed up quickly. A blister started to form on the heel of my left foot. I covered it with a one inch piece of duct tape. The tape stayed on for over a week and when I pulled it off, the blister was gone. On the hike overall, I had good luck with blisters. I had few of them, and when I did, I would stick duct tape on them and ignore them.

I hiked thirteen miles and found a good camping spot beside the trail. The next morning started with a nasty climb from 2,800 feet to 4,450 feet and covered eleven miles. It wasn't all uphill but it sure felt like it. I passed a middle aged couple only about 1/8th of the way into the day's climb. She was sprawled on the ground looking morose and totally exhausted. He was sitting in the shade of a tree, looking at his map, and glancing at the climb ahead. It was a steep one for about a mile. It looked like reality had collided with their dreams. My guess is they called their thru-hike quits at Neels Gap. I continued on and reached Neels Gap by 5:00 pm. I planned to get some snacks at the outfitters, hike another couple of miles, and find a place to put my tent. I had hiked fourteen miles.

The outfitter's store at Neels Gap provided a real service. Many times when thru-hikers reached Neels Gap their packs weighed 40 to 50 pounds and sometimes a lot more than that. The outfitters gave these heavy packs a shake-down and took out all the non- essentials. (Of course, they sold a lot of light weight gear, too.) Then they showed the hikers how to pack the pack with the right weight distribution. Hikers who followed their recommendations had a much easier hike. It's a lot easier carrying a 25 pound pack with food and water from Georgia to Maine than a 40 pound pack.

As I left Neels Gap I stopped at a forest service bulletin board at the trailhead. These bulletin boards tell how to prevent forest fires, filter your water, leave no trace, how not to attract bears and they have hiker alerts. There was a Forest Ranger Alert: [Rogue Bear! It has no fear of people. No camping from Neels Gap to Tray Gap – a total of 25 miles. Hikers have to stay in shelters in this area.] From what I learned later, on more than one occasion, this bear had gone after hiker's packs while they were taking breaks.

I looked at my Thru-Hikers' Companion Guidebook. The next shelter was eight miles away. Great! It's 5:30 pm and I'm tired. I've got eight more miles to hike and I don't want to be hiking in the dark with a rogue bear around. I got my butt in gear! I made it to the shelter by 8:15 pm and still had a little daylight left. After a 22 mile day, I was beat.

This shelter had the most aggressive mice of any that I encountered. I was never bothered by mice coming after my food while I was around it. They usually came out at night when I was in my sleeping bag. As soon as I started emptying my food bag on the picnic table, these mice were trying to get at it. I would brush them away and they would come right back. Since I had the shelter to myself, I put up the tent in the shelter with just the netting and ate my dinner zipped up inside. That night I slept fitfully. The thought of a rogue bear was on my mind and the constant sound of scurrying mice was distracting. At one time I turned on my flashlight and three mice were crawling on the netting.

I was getting low on food and the next supply town was Helen, Georgia. Helen was nine miles east on Highway 75. I had no luck hitch hiking so I decided to walk. At least most of it was downhill. It started to rain for the first time during my hike. I put on my rain jacket. It began to pour. There was very little shoulder to walk on. I was getting sprayed by passing cars and particularly the trucks. It continued to rain all nine miles. I picked up a couple of ticks along the way. Fortunately, I could feel them working their way up my leg. This may sound weird, but I remember thinking: "Is this fun or what!" and laughing.

I finally made it into town and stopped at a Wendy's. I was soaking wet. When I finished eating, I stood up to leave and there was a puddle of water on my chair. The nicest lady who worked at Wendy's came over, wiped it down, gave me a big smile, and wished me a good day.

Helen, Georgia was a theme town. All the businesses and a lot of the houses had a Swiss Chalet look. This was a Saturday during tourist season and it was crowded and hectic. It had a good grocery store with a wonderful selection for a trail mix. There were bins of dehydrated banana sluices, dried apricots, almonds, cashews, peanuts, granola, M&M's, malted balls (my favorite since I was a kid), and chocolate covered everything. I went wild! I must have gotten ten pounds of trail mix alone. I paid the price carrying it the next few days, but I sure did enjoy it.

I groaned under the extra pack weight on the nine mile uphill road walk back to the Trail. I didn't think I would get a ride and headed uphill facing traffic which I felt was safer. At least it wasn't raining. I was resigned to the fact that I would get to the trailhead around 8:00 pm and put up my tent in the dark. After I had hiked a mile, a guy in a beat up pickup truck yelled over and asked if I needed a ride. Sure! I scampered across the road and hopped in. It was a pleasure listening to the old truck strain on the long uphill grade. Delbert even gave me a can of beer. I put it in my backpack and thoroughly enjoyed it after I had set up camp - in the daylight.

That night there was a big thunderstorm. My tent held up beautifully to the pounding rain. I had a good night's sleep and the next morning enjoyed the fresh smell of the forest after a rain. There were trees in this area that had a profusion of bright orange flowers. As I started my hike, I crossed a little stream with crystal clear water. While I was filling my water bottles, I met the first person I was going to hike with on my journey. His name was John. He had hiked the entire AT with his wife in 2006. He enjoyed it so much he was doing a three week section hike of the AT just to re- live the experience. He was 62, just like me. He had heavy braces on both knees and his gait was awkward but he was tall and covered ground fast. I was starting to get my trail legs by this time, but his pace on up hills kept me gasping for breath. I wasn't about to let him pull ahead of me, though. He was a natural storyteller and the hours went by fast. He was also a good listener and I was glad to be talking to an experienced hiker. The best advice he gave me had to do with water. I had decided I wasn't going to filter my water during my AT hike. He suggested I look out for beaver ponds above my water source. Beaver waste carries an organism that needs to be filtered. I followed this religiously, usually waiting until I was high in the mountains before getting water and I never got giardia or anything else.

John stopped at a shelter where he was going to wait for a group he was hiking with and I continued on my way. I found a campsite two miles before the Georgia-North Carolina state line. The next morning I bagged my first state: Georgia down, thirteen more to go.

This was a beautiful area. I especially remember the birds. It was early May and they were staking their territories. Such a variety of melodies filled the air. There were rhododendrons galore. Sometimes they were so thick they overlapped the trail forming a tunnel. It must have been stunning when they were in bloom.

I would say by the time I reached North Carolina I had my trail legs. I was pleasantly tired at the end of each day, but not overly tired. I was hiking faster and was up to about eighteen miles a day. My appetite was ravenous and the trail mix was helping with that. It was dense with the calories I needed, nutritious, and tasted good. A friend of my sister's, Karen Bond, gave me a fanny pack and I can't count how many times over the course of my thru-hike I completely filled it with trail mix and emptied it.

There was a small sign on a tree that marked the Georgia/North Carolina border. I think the North Carolina chapter of the Appalachian Trail Club or ATC wanted to show how tough they were. Every state seemed to want to do this. The next nine miles were very steep. The elevation went from 3,825' to 5,498'. About three miles into this torture I pulled into the Muskrat Creek shelter to catch my breath.

Shelters along the Trail were spaced about seven to twelve miles apart. In age, they could go back as far as the 1920's to this year. Most were made of thick sturdy logs and were practically indestructible, although hikers over the years have managed to burn some down. A few were made of stone. Ninety-nine percent of shelters were three sided structures. If the wind was blowing from the wrong direction it could be awfully cold and drafty. Shelters were about eight feet deep. Some had bunks. Most of the time, you slept on an elevated wooden floor. Sometimes you slept with your head next to the entrance of the shelter, other times in the opposite direction. The number of people that a shelter could accommodate ranged from six to twenty plus. The average shelter held eight people. Shelters ranged from dark, dirty, and depressing to three stories with skylights. Usually there was a picnic table in front. People cooked their food on these tables and socialized there. Tables had numerous burn marks from the portable stoves. The floors of the shelters also had scorch marks where hikers had cooked during windy, rainy, cold weather. If you were lucky, there would be an overhang to shelter the picnic table from the rain.

Each shelter had a shelter journal. A hiker would come into a shelter, write the date, and make an entry. A lot of the time it was about the day's hike or the weather, but it could be about anything. Some entries were humorous, some were angry, some were weird. It was a way of reading about what was happening with hikers ahead of you and communicating with hikers behind you. Over a period of time on the Trail, these journals took on a life of their own. They became miniature soap operas. Most hikers stopped at almost all the shelters just to read the shelter journals and write in them.

It rained steadily for the next two days. I had on my red hiking shirt, fleece pullover, raincoat, and gloves. I was hiking as fast as I could in the conditions and getting cold. I saw maybe three hikers the first day. The second day the conditions were even worse. It was cold. The wind was fierce. The rain was pounding. I knew I had the trail all to myself. Wrong! I was startled to see three ladies my age or older heading toward me. They greeted me like a long lost friend. They were laughing and having a great time. One of the ladies, who had to be approaching 70, was on her last section of the AT. She had started hiking the AT by sections twenty years earlier. She had ten miles to go to have hiked the entire Appalachian Trail. She was really excited. They wanted to stay and talk and I did for a few minutes, but I was starting to shiver. Their obvious joy of hiking picked up my spirits.

I continued on to Wesser Bald Observatory. It had 360 degree views with little plaques showing which mountains you were looking at. I was looking at dense fog and could see about ten feet. I hiked for three more hours and found a great little camping spot. It was a level spot for a change, so I wasn't sliding right or left, up or down in my sleeping bag. It was next to a stream. I try to get close enough to a stream so the sound of the flowing water blocks out any background noises. Sometimes if I get it just right I can fall into an undisturbed deep sleep. I got it just right.

The next morning I hiked three miles to the Natahala Outdoor Center or the NOC. I watched white water rafters shooting through the rapids. It looked fun.

After getting heavily stocked with food I headed to Cheoah Bald. I left the NOC at 2:00 pm. My guidebook showed Cheoah Bald to be a little over eight miles. I should have looked at the elevation changes. It started at 1,723' and rose to 5,062' in eight miles. Of all the hikes I had on my trip, this one stands out in my memory as one of the toughest. It kept going up and up, hour after hour. I passed a lot of people. Three-quarters of the way up, I stopped at a cool little spring. I was so thirsty I emptied my 32 ounce water bottle and almost emptied it a second time. That water was wonderful.

I passed four thru-hikers in their early twenties. They kept trying to re-pass me. I was in a rhythm and had a good pace going. The climb was steep and didn't let up. They would get right on my tail and make noises like they were ready to pass me, then they would take a cigarette break. This happened a couple of times. By the end of the day I was over an hour ahead of them.

I reached Cheoah Bald at 6:00 pm. What a lovely spot. I had it all to myself. The views were incredible. There was nothing but forest in every direction. I found a level area to put my tent. It was a warm night so I used the netting on my tent without the cover. I lay down on my air mattress with just my shorts on. Endorphins were cascading through my body as it cooled down from the day's exhausting climb. I felt great! Bugs were buzzing around the tent trying to get in. I was completely relaxed. I put my hands behind my head and looked up at the sky. I saw a beautiful sunset. Stars gradually started to appear. Soon the night sky was alive with twinkling stars. Way in the distance I could see the lights of small towns. It was quiet and peaceful and relaxing. It is one of my best memories.

2 THE SMOKIES

My next day's destination was an eighteen mile hike to a campsite two miles before Fontana Dam. Fontana Dam Visitor's Center is where you register to start your hike through the Great Smoky Mountain National Park.

"On Top Of Old Smoky. All Covered With Snow. I lost My True Lover. For A Courtin' Too Slow."

I always wanted to hike in the Smokies. This was a healthy, vibrant forest. It was also a busy park with over nine million visitors annually and over 400 bears.

At the Visitor's Center I filled out my Backcountry Camping Permit. You can't tent in the park, you have to use the shelters. I was dreading this. I have my copy of the permit in front of me as I write this: May 9th, Mollies Ridge Shelter. May 10th, Double Spring Shelter. May 11th, Pecks Corner Shelter. May 12th, Davenport Gap Shelter. It was an ambitious agenda. Many people take up to a week or more to hike the Smokies. The elevations were high with a lot of long climbs and descents and the terrain was rugged. I checked my food supply. I had four days of food. The town of Fontana was a tourist town and everything was pricey so I decided to skip the re-supply. (Not one of my better decisions).

Hiking up to Mollies Ridge shelter, dark clouds started moving in and I heard the first rumbling of thunder. Soon there were flashes of lightning. I would count the seconds until I heard the Boom. The intervals were getting shorter. Light rain turned into a downpour. FLASH! BOOM! "Woah! That was close!" I was down in the trees and not on an exposed ridge so I kept moving. I was pumping gallons of adrenaline. My mantra was: "No ridgeline. No ridgeline. No ridgeline. No ridgeline."

"Shit! The trail is heading to a ridgeline!"

FLASH! BOOM!! It's amazing how fast you can hike in a thunderstorm with the wind and rain slapping you around on a slippery, muddy, pathway with steep, rocky, climbs.

I reached the ridgeline. If I had been exposed on the ridgeline I think I would have stopped and waited out the storm. Fortunately, there were tall trees around. The lightning continued to flash, and thunder loudly reverberated through the mountains. My mantra had changed: "I hate this! I hate this! I hate this!" I practically jogged across the ridgeline. It was only about three minutes but it seemed like forever. I was waiting to feel the buzz of an imminent lightning strike. Finally I was off the ridgeline and heading back down the mountain. The thunderstorm slowly moved out of the area and I began to relax and unwind. "Crack! Boom!" One more time just for good measure and it was gone. I HATE thunderstorms! Always have. Always will.

During the storm I passed a father, mother, and two teenaged kids walking back to their car. They had probably been on a picnic earlier in the day and still had an hour to go to get to their car. They were only wearing shorts and short sleeved shirts and were absolutely soaked. Dad gave me a sheepish: "Hello." If looks could kill: Mom and the two kids were shooting daggers at Dad!

I reached Mollies Ridge shelter at 5:30 pm. It was a fairly big shelter that could hold up to twelve people. I was grateful for the large tarp rigged over the front to keep out the cold wind. I was the last hiker in for the night. There were eight of us. There was a couple about my age who looked very tired, a man in his fifties working on some nasty blisters, a teacher spending her summer vacation trying to hike as far as Pennsylvania, a couple in their mid-twenties, and an idiot who bragged about carrying a 70 pound pack.

At this time I wasn't using a stove so that I could save weight. I ate my light weight dried food while everyone else brought out their stoves and started cooking wonderful smelling concoctions. By 8:30 pm when most of us were ready for bed, 70# Idiot decided to cook his dinner. He pulled out a MRE from his pack. Meals Ready to Eat. They are used by our soldiers. They are heavy to carry but you eat well. His was Beef Enchiladas with fruit, vegetables and dessert. There was even a cup with coffee crystals. When he added water, it heated the coffee to the right temperature without a stove. The coffee smelled wonderful. The enchiladas smelled even better. My stomach was growling. I was already starting to ration my food so that I could make it through the Smokies. Wingo Idiot!

Somebody yelled: "BEAR!!!" Everyone headed to the front of the shelter and peered around the tarp. "He's coming this way!" "Yell! Bang some pans!" "OK he's moving back." "Here he comes again!" "Oh! God! Everybody Yell!" "OK. He's moved back to the edge of the trees. He's just staying there." "Get your camera." "I'm taking a video of him right now."

"Wow! That's a big bear!" "What if he comes into the shelter?"

While this was taking place, I was in my sleeping bag. I figured they were making enough noise to keep the bear at bay. I had seen more than enough bears on my hikes over the years. I didn't want to see a bear on this thru-hike. The teacher came over to me and showed me the video she had taken of the bear. Her zoom lens had done a great job. It looked like you could reach out and touch that big bear. His nose was up in the air and he was smelling those enchiladas. Bears have a powerful sense of smell. It was probably driving him crazy. He stayed on the periphery of the shelter for a few more minutes and moved on. Everyone was wound up, talking excitedly, and peering out of the shelter for the next hour. I didn't get a lot of sleep that night. I'm not used to sleeping around that many people and so close. I could smell the breath of the lady sleeping next to me.

I reached Russell Field shelter at 9:00 the next morning. It was completely enclosed with fencing. The hikers who had been there the night before also had bear activity during the night. I just missed seeing a mother bear and her cubs. Everyone at the shelter was still excited.

As the shelters in the Smokies are improved, they stop using the fencing. It was having exactly the wrong effect. Hikers inside the fence were enticing bears to the fence with food so they could get good pictures of them. Can you believe that? There were too many bears in Georgia, North Carolina, Tennessee, and Virginia who were not afraid of people. That's not natural. I didn't feel comfortable tenting in those states. In Maine, New Hampshire, Vermont, Massachusetts, and Connecticut, I saw few bears and when they saw me they took off like a rocket. I enjoyed tenting in those states.

From Russell Field shelter there was a strenuous two hour climb to Rocky Top. At times the pathway wandered through long abandoned apple orchards. From Rocky Top I could see far away towns and lakes. There had been a pathway here for many years. Many of the big rocks had names and dates chiseled into them; some dating as far back as the 1820's.

One hundred and eighty years ago there was a person standing right where I was standing, chiseling his name into the rock. What was his life like back then? Did he even realize that for hundreds of years people would be reading his name that he had boldly chiseled into the rock?

I continued climbing to Thunderhead Mountain. It was windy at the peak and there was a light drizzle. As I began to descend, it was muddy and slippery in places. I was picking my way carefully. I came to a part of the pathway that stopped me in my tracks. It was on the side of the mountain. Right next to the pathway was a sheer drop. Way down. Like if you fall you are dead, down. Just looking at the extent of the drop-off took my breath away. I had to take my time and figure this one out. There were rocks of all sizes on the pathway. The area with the steepest drop-off turned to the right as it steeply descended. The footing was tricky. It was raining and the rocks on the pathway were slippery. I needed to be holding onto bigger rocks as I was descending, that meant tossing my hiking poles to the pathway below. I wanted to make sure I didn't accidentally lean toward the drop off and have my pack weight carry me over the side. This was scary. It had my full attention. My heart was pumping! A cold wind was blowing. I could hear droplets of rain pattering against my raincoat. I knew if I screwed up I was dead. I stopped, looked around, and thought: "I'm Loving This!" I took a deep breath, exhaled slowly, and ever so slowly made my descent. I was stretched to the limits of my ability. When I was past the obstacle, I let out a long sigh of relief and felt the tension in my body relax.

In the next hour the weather began to improve. By noon it had turned into a beautiful day. I passed green meadows covered with colorful wildflowers. Bees were buzzing industriously. The smell of rich earth and fragrant flowers filled the air. The hiking was delightful. I made it to Double Spring shelter by 5:00 pm - a 19 mile day. It was a bright new shelter with skylights and an upper loft. It had an enclosed area for the picnic table. It started raining right after I arrived and rained most of the night.

I left the shelter the next morning at 7:30. I had a 21 mile hike to get to Peck's Corner shelter. The Trail passed Clingman's Dome. At 6,643' it was the highest point on the Appalachian Trail. It was an observation tower with a wide spiraling walkway that led to the top. It looked right out of the Jetson's. At the top were 360 degree views that probably would have been impressive if not for the dense fog and drizzle. I continued on my way.

Within an hour I ran into my first trail magic. Trail magic can be many things, but often it is food and drink left beside the Trail in a Styrofoam container just for thru-hikers. I had trail magic many times during my hike and greatly appreciated it. The timing of the trail magic couldn't have been better. I was running low on energy. My trail magic was a package of Pop Tarts and an energy drink. I hadn't had anything caffeinated since I started my thru-hike and that drink hit me like a ton of bricks. It was one of those really high energy drinks. I took off like a rocket, powering my way up the mountain and kept going that way for three hours. There wasn't much visibility. It was foggy with a stiff breeze. Sometimes there was a light drizzle. I did a lot of ridge walking where the pathway was the actual boundary between North Carolina and Tennessee. There were sheer drops on either side of the trail. The views must have been spectacular. I heard from other hikers that they were. I passed an emaciated man high on the ridge. He had on a small food belt and some water. He was wearing a thin, long sleeved shirt and covered with a blanket. It was cold and breezy. He was carrying a bible and probably on a spiritual quest. I said a quick: "Hi" and kept going. I reached Peck's Corner shelter at 6:00 pm. There were fifteen people at the shelter and a lot of them were in their 40's, 50's, and

60's. All age groups seemed to be well represented on the Appalachian Trail. One guy was a hellacious, non-stop snorer. The person next to him would nudge him and he would let out a "Snort!" and go right on snoring.

The next day I hiked 23 miles passing Davenport Gap shelter at 4:00 pm and heading out of the Great Smoky Mountain National Park. When I knew I was within two miles of where I was going to spend the night, I ate the handful of trail mix that was all the food I had left. I lost some weight in the Smokies but I was soft around the middle and could afford to lose it.

My destination was Standing Bear Hostel. Curtis, the owner, greeted me and showed me around the place. There was a log cabin bunkhouse and other cabins on the ten acre property. It had a rustic charm. The central location was a fire ring with benches around it. It was 5:30 pm and the beer was already flowing. Curtis was feeling no pain. He took me to the bunkhouse and let me drop off my gear. He pointed to the outhouse and told me that everyone peed behind the bunkhouse next to the road. That road was fairly busy, too. I had to time it right a couple of times. There was a garage that was turned into a camp store. It was on the honor system. You listed the food items with their prices, totaled it up, put your trail name on the front of the envelope and put the money inside. The selection wasn't the greatest so I bought enough food for two days which was enough to get to Hot Springs, North Carolina and a good re-supply. I was starving. I devoured two cans of chili con carne and a can of ravioli. I was tired after four grueling days in the Smokies. The bunk house was clean. I had a soft bed with clean sheets and a blanket. After taking a much needed shower, I went to bed and had a good night's sleep.

The next morning at breakfast I visited with some of the other hikers before heading out. One of them was Fletch. I have been asked if there were any "characters" on the trail. Fletch is the first hiker I met that the word "character" came to mind. He was a nice guy. Forty-one years old although when I was asked to guess his age I guessed thirty. He had a long ponytail and was cheerful and sincere. He was a gadget man and had all kinds of electronic gadgets in his backpack. With a gleam in his eye of the true zealot he would describe them in detail if given the chance. The first time I saw him he was describing all the features of his watch. That took about ten minutes. Remember that I mentioned how the outfitters at Neels Gap provide a real service by taking heavy packs and getting rid of all the non-essentials? When Fletch got to Neels Gap his pack weighed sixty pounds. When he left, it weighed sixty-five pounds! At Standing Bear Hostel he was packing two t-bone steaks and a quart of milk in a glass container. The thought of carrying that is enough to give a lightweight backpacker cold sweats and palpitations. After purchasing a huge amount of food, he would spend the night watching for bears with his arm around his food bag and a machete in his other hand. If there was ever a lull in the conversation at night at any campsite whether it was in Virginia, Pennsylvania, or Maine, all I had to say was: "Did you ever meet Fletch?" Everyone had a Fletch story. I was glad to see that he summited Katahdin on the 8th of October.

I left Standing Bear Hostel and planned a take-it-easy day of fifteen miles. It was a beautiful day. I dawdled along taking frequent breaks and chatting with people on the Trail. In the evening I climbed Max Patch Bald. It was a big impressive bald that was high enough for views in all directions. I met a young couple who were tented in the trees on the edge of the bald and had hiked back to the top hand in hand. The sun was just beginning to turn a pinkish red on the horizon. They looked very much in love. They asked me to take their picture. That picture will bring back treasured memories.

By 7:30 pm I reached Roaring Fork shelter. It was about two miles from the Max Patch summit. Time Bomb, his wife Thimble, Aqua Fresh, and Chinese Tourist were already there. I met Time Bomb and Thimble at the Standing Bear Hostel. They had saved money and quit their jobs so they could hike the AT. He was a salesman and she was a physician's assistant. Aqua Fresh and Chinese Tourist were hiking together. They were in their early twenties. Aqua Fresh had to be 6'8" and Chinese Tourist was 6'4".

For dinner I had a can of Pringles Potato Chips. As I was sitting in the shelter eating my potato chips I saw a couple of mice dart by. I said to the others: "Man, I don't want to mess with these mice tonight. I'm going to tent instead." The shelter had three designated camping spots. Mine was a level area with small boards around it about thirty yards from the shelter. There was even a bear cable five feet from the tent site. Great!

My plan was to put my food bag and any other items that might have a bear attracting odor into a 33 gallon plastic garbage bag and into my backpack. After seeing the thick bear cable I knew that once I hoisted the backpack up the bear cable it would be totally secure.

I set up my tent, changed into my camp clothes, brushed my teeth, secured my backpack, and got into my sleeping bag. It had been an enjoyable day. I drifted into a peaceful sleep.

Around 11:00 pm I heard a big commotion at the shelter. The first thing to cross my mind was that it must be a bear. There was a thick sturdy bear cable about twenty feet from the shelter hung between two big trees. Food bags were put on hooks and hoisted up by a cable line securely attached five feet above the base of the tree. The food bags were a good fifteen feet above the ground. No bear could possibly get to them but this one was apparently trying.

I heard a lot of loud yelling, banging of pots and pans, even a log being thumped on the ground. After about fifteen minutes the sounds died down and then stopped. I figured they had probably scared the bear away. I listened closely for twigs being snapped or any other sign that the bear might be headed my way. After a while my eyes grew heavy and I fell back asleep.

I had a dream. In this dream a bear was crashing through the forest and heading toward my tent. Just before he reached my tent, I woke up. My heart was beating rapidly. I looked around and realized it was only a dream. Whew! What a relief! I closed my eyes and started to drift back to sleep.

Within minutes I heard LOUD crashing sounds. Branches were being broken off of bushes, and pieces of wood on the ground were snapping loudly! A bear was heading right toward my tent! He was making a low grumbling sound. He stopped at the bear cable which was only five feet from my tent, gave a low grunt, and pushed down on the cable with his full weight. I could hear the cable vibrating but it didn't break. With a louder grunt he pushed down even harder. This time the cable snapped.

With trepidation, I grabbed my flashlight, unzipped the tent, and headed out. Five feet in front of me was a Really Big Smelly Black Bear! I flashed my flashlight at him and he turned and looked at me. I yelled at the top of my lungs: "GET OUT OF HERE! GET OUT OF HERE! GET OUT OF HERE!" He moved back about ten feet. The backpack was miraculously still on the sagging cable. A broken cable line dangled down five feet from the ground. The bear hadn't gotten the food so he started coming forward again. He headed to the dangling cable line and pulled the line to shake the backpack loose. With as much menace as I could muster, I yelled: "GET OUT OF HERE!" He moved back, although not as far back. He almost immediately moved forward again and now he was standing up. Damn he was big!

Chinese Tourist appeared by my side; all six foot four, two hundred pounds of him. We were both yelling at him and Chinese Tourist had a shaft he had fashioned with a big knife attached to it. He had his headlight on the bear and was jabbing at him to move him back. The bear was standing his ground and starting to huff. While Chinese Tourist was distracting the bear, I put on my shoes, grabbed my sleeping bag, and facing the bear, we slowly moved away and back to the shelter. I could hear the bear trying to shake the backpack off of its hook. After a while he gave up and left.

I have been asked what my emotions were while this was happening: I realized I was in a life threatening situation. I was hyper-alert and focused. I was determined not to show fear but I could feel my heart beating rapidly. I focused on yelling at the bear and getting him to leave. When he didn't leave the second time I yelled at him, I realized I had better get out of there. It was a great relief to see Chinese Tourist show up. That is a brave man! He came to my aid in the darkness of the night knowing he was going to confront a bear, and he came anyway. I thanked him gratefully.

The bear had broken the cable earlier at the shelter when I heard all the commotion. He then proceeded to slash all four food bags and eat the food right in front of Time Bomb, Thimble, Aqua Fresh, and Chinese Tourist. That bear had absolutely no fear of humans. Everyone was wound up and we talked into the night, wondering if the bear would come back.

At first light Aqua Fresh heard some noise: "Wingo. Get up. I think I hear the bear over by your tent." Sure enough we could barely make out the shape of the bear. He was trying to get into the tent. I heard a ripping sound and my tent poles snapping as he put his full weight on the tent. We didn't try to yell the bear away. When he was finished, he sauntered leisurely up the Trail, totally in charge; a surly look on his face. We went over to see the damage. Totaled! The poles were broken. The bottom slashed. My sleeping pad had bear claw slashes on it and a hole in it the size of my fist. There were bite marks on my Thru-Hikers Companion Guidebook. There was nothing in my tent that could have attracted that bear. He couldn't get to my food. He was pissed! My tent paid the price.

The group tried to salvage anything from their destroyed food bags. There wasn't much left although Thimble was delighted that the bear hadn't eaten her five month supply of birth control pills. She had a good sense of humor: "Can you imagine what would have happened if the bear had eaten my birth control pills? I can see myself calling my doctor and asking to have my prescription refilled. The doctor says: 'Didn't I just give you a prescription for five months of birth control pills?' Uh. You're not going to believe this............"

3 HOT SPRINGS, NORTH CAROLINA

We all packed up and headed out together. Our destination was Hot Springs, North Carolina. Eventually I pulled ahead of them although I did see them again in Hot Springs. I was glad to see that Time Bomb and Thimble summited Katahdin in October and Chinese Tourist summited on the 8th of October with Fletch.

The Appalachian Trail went right through Hot Springs. It felt kind of odd following the white Appalachian Trail blazes through town. I reached town at 5:00 pm. I could feel the lack of sleep from the night before. I didn't have a tent so I decided to stay at another hostel. The one recommended was Elmer's Sunnybank Inn. The owner was a man in his 70's. He had been an activist in the area for many years. The hostel was his old Victorian house dating back to at least the 1840's. Elmer had restored it beautifully. Most of the furniture was antique and looked expensive. The stairway was made of a dark walnut. The living room with its decorations and antiques had the look and feel of the nineteenth century.

The dinner was vegetarian but the word was that you never left Elmer's table hungry. There were sixteen of us seated around the dining room table. We introduced ourselves and told a little bit about ourselves. The conversation was lively and the food was delicious. It started with a thick salad with a variety of ingredients. I had a creamy, cheesy dressing that was the best I have ever tasted. I thought this might be the whole meal so I had seconds and thirds on a big plate. The next course was vegetarian lasagna. I had seconds of that, too. Dessert was a homemade apple pie with ice cream. Excellent! Just as we were finishing our dinner someone mentioned there had been a bear encounter on the trail the night before. I had a captivated audience for about ten minutes. After dinner, people congregated in the living room to listen to a good pianist. I was tired so I went to bed. I was lucky to have a room of my own. Once I had gotten into bed a loud thunderstorm passed through. As I watched rain droplets flowing down the window pane I was grateful to be in a nice warm bed.

As I was leaving town I stopped at a little place that served mocha lattes. I always looked forward to a mocha latte in each town that I re-supplied. The waitress was new on the job and wanted to make it just right. She gave a big sigh of relief when I complimented her. We chatted while I sipped my latte. She also worked at the outfitters in Hot Springs. I told her about the bear encounter.

"Yea." She said. "That big old bear has been messing with people for over a year. We sell a lot of pots and pans to people who left their campsites in a hurry."

I saw eighteen bears during my thru-hike. The bear at the Roaring Fork shelter was by far the biggest. Apparently he had been successfully stealing food in a 20 mile area each night for over a year. Food bags usually have a lot of food in them. This bear was huge. He had absolutely no fear of people. He was skilled at breaking cables and stealing food bags. He knew how to break ropes that were tied to a tree to secure food bags. He was so knowledgeable that re-location wouldn't have worked. It was a matter of time before he hurt someone.

I tried to salvage my tent as best I could. I cut out all the netting and patched up the slashed area with a lot of duct tape. I kept six stakes. It was about two pounds lighter and I could feel the difference in the weight when I carried my pack. I called it my tarp tent. I planned to buy a new tent when I reached my sister's house near Waynesboro, Virginia. I replaced the sleeping pad with a self-inflating mattress. It was a pound heavier than the sleeping pad, but my tarp tent was two pounds lighter. I loved the new air mattress. With the sleeping pad I could feel whatever was beneath me - roots, twigs, pebbles. The air mattress kept me above those irritants.

From Hot Springs, North Carolina to Waynesboro, Virginia - 581 miles - I started using the shelters. I wasn't thrilled at the idea, but looking back, it turned out to be a good thing. I became much more social.

I arrived at the Spring Mountain shelter at 6:00 pm. No one was there. The bear encounter was still fresh on my mind and I wanted to be around people that night. For about a week the loud crashing sound of the bear heading toward my tent bothered me. After that I was fine. Finally three section hikers came in at 7:00 pm. I enjoyed their company as much as any on the trail. They were from Illinois. Each year they hiked different sections of the AT. They had been doing this for years. Fire Starter was the youngest at 42. He was the quiet one of the group. He earned his trail name and kept a great blaze going. Bull Shooter was in his mid-fifties. He was a pharmacist. As his trail name implies, he was verbal. Sarge was a 58 year old postal worker. He liked to give the orders. They obviously enjoyed each other's company. They included me in their group almost immediately. They were on an adventure and were enjoying it to the hilt. They had been hiking for a week and had one day left. We sat around the fire that night and bull shooted.

Spring Mountain shelter was built in 1938 and had not been renovated. The depth of the shelter was only six feet. Even my head was close to hanging over the edge and I'm 5'8". It must have been miserable for all the six footers. It rained throughout the night. There were advantages to sleeping in shelters. You don't have to pack up a wet tent in the morning or carry the extra weight of a wet tent. The sound of raindrops on the tin roof of a shelter always made it sound like it was raining harder than it actually was. When it was raining hard the sound was impressive.

The next morning Fire Starter had a crackling fire going. A cold front was coming through and it was chilly. The fire felt good. For the next three days it became colder with each passing day. A lot of each day was spent hiking in fog or light drizzle. Walking in fog was a treat. I almost never saw any other hikers on a foggy day. I had the forest all to myself. I was in my own little world. Sometimes the fog was so thick I had to concentrate to stay on the right path. The mist created an atmosphere that was quiet and relaxing. Eerily quiet - no birds, chipmunks, squirrels, bees, bugs, or any sounds.

Since I was no longer tenting, I could figure my exact mileage for each day. My mileage for the next five days was 21, 19, 22, 22, and 21.6. The border between North Carolina and Tennessee followed all of this mileage. I might be in a shelter in Tennessee one night and in a shelter in North Carolina the next.

When I reached Flint Mountain shelter that evening, there was Rocky. I sat next to her at dinner at Elmer's hostel. She was in her early thirties and was taking a leave of absence from her job as a counselor to troubled kids. She worked with these kids in the Rocky Mountains in Colorado. Nice lady.

The only other person at the shelter was a man in his forties who had hurt his knee and was getting off of the Trail the next day. He was an authority on everything. It got old real quick. I was in my sleeping bag by 8:30 pm and soon sleeping peacefully when I heard: SSSSNNNNNXXXXX!!! The guy next to me was lying on his back and snoring. You would have to hear this to believe it. He would make an enormous inhale which was powerful enough to vibrate the floor. He had apnea so he would stop breathing. I'm going: "C'mon! C'mon! Breathe!" Then he would let loose with a loud: SSSSNNNNOOOORRRRKKKK!!! The floor would vibrate again. This went on all night. I asked Rocky the next morning if she had gotten any sleep. She said she had worn earplugs and still couldn't sleep. There are some people who shouldn't sleep in shelters. He was one of them.

The next day's hiking was in fog until around 2:00 pm and it drizzled the rest of the day. It was cold and breezy and I was slowly losing body heat. By the time I reached the shelter where I was going to spend the night, I was shivering. My hands were numb from the cold and my lips were so numb I was slurring my words. I took out a tuna packet, ripped the top off with my teeth, and slid the tuna up the packet while I ate it. That's the only way I could eat it. My hands were useless. I knew I had to get out of my wet muddy socks and shoes and out of my wet clothes right away. It was only 7:00 pm but I put on dry clothes and got into my sleeping bag. I was shivering for at least an hour. It took a long time to regain my body heat. My feet stayed cold until early morning.

The next morning was cold. My fingers were like ice cycles when I was making breakfast. They were painful when I was packing my backpack. That reinforced my belief that my thru-hike needed to be a fast one. I didn't think I would be able to handle the cold in the mountains of New Hampshire and Maine in September.

Rocky was hiking about my speed and I enjoyed talking with her in the morning and at the end of the day. She would always ask me how far I was going. We ended the day at the same shelter for four days in a row which was unusual. I'm sure Rocky had an excellent hike. She had an effervescent personality, always upbeat and positive. She made friends easily. She could put in good mileage which left her time to enjoy all the town stops. Rocky summited Katahdin in early October.

After the third day of rain and fog it started to clear. The next two days were crystal clear and sunny. I had to work hard hiking these steep mountains but the rewards were awesome. One of my favorite balds was called Beauty Spot. From the top it seemed like I could see forever. I could visualize Julie Andrews on this bald, singing "The Hills Are Alive With The Sound Of Music" and doing her little pirouette.

This was just a beautiful area to hike in. One part was dominated by tall pine trees. The ground was carpeted with fragrant pine needles that made the pathway soft and cushioned the sound of my footsteps. I particularly liked the soft part. I caught up to Easy Strider. She was about twenty, tall, attractive, and looked fit. We walked together for a while and then I took a break. The day before, she had been on Beauty Spot at a hiker feed. Hikers from previous years had grilled hamburgers and hot dogs. Fifty people spent the night tenting on Beauty Spot and partying. Easy Strider looked like she was paying the price. I passed her again on an uphill climb and she looked miserable. "When will this ever stop going uphill?" She moaned.

I made it to Clyde Smith shelter by 4:00 pm, which was early for me. No one was there. There was a waterfall nearby and I had a chance to fill my wash container and clean myself and my clothes. Heading back to the shelter I felt clean and refreshed. Easy Strider made it in at 5:00 pm. She was hiking with a group of people her age and they started trickling in. I wasn't included in much of the conversation, however, they were all nice and I wasn't excluded. Two of the hikers in the group started a fire, opened cans of Campbell's Beans and Franks, and heated the cans over the fire. You know what that's leading up to, and it did, all through the night. Groan.

I met this group at shelters on two other occasions, got to know them a little better each time, and like them even more. Easy Strider started her thru-hike staying mainly in her hammock at night. Hammocks are nice. I was tempted to get one. All you do is tie them between two trees and you can sleep almost anywhere. The interiors are like tents, they have bug netting, and only weigh about two pounds. Easy Strider was sleeping in her hammock one night when she was awakened by a bear sniffing her butt! Easy Strider now stayed almost exclusively in shelters.

My gosh! The gamut of emotions this group displayed. If one wasn't feeling good, you heard about it. Blisters, ailments, upset stomach, diarrhea, personality clashes -- you heard about it. One of the hikers wanted to quit and everyone was trying to talk him out of it. They were all in a depressed mood. It would have driven me crazy being around a group for too long.

My hike from Clyde Smith shelter to Apple House shelter covered 22 strenuous miles with hard climbs. It was one of my best hiking days. These were the Roan Mountains. There were three spectacular balds that day. The elevation went above 6,000' a couple of times and much of the hike was above tree line. The weather couldn't have been better. Usually on a bald you get pelted with wind. This was a calm day, probably one of the best visibility days of the year for the area.

Climbing to the first 6,000' peak, the mountainside was covered with rhododendron. From there I went down, down, down to Carver's Gap, then up, up, up to Grassy Ridge, down, down, down again to Yellow Mountain Gap. (Isn't this fun?) Continental soldiers passed through Yellow Mountain Gap during the Revolutionary War.

Yellow Mountain Gap was where I saw the most impressive shelter on the Trail. Overmountain shelter was a large red converted barn which could comfortably sleep twenty-five people. There was a gently flowing stream nearby and beautiful views down the valley. Unfortunately I passed it at 2:00 pm and it was too early to call it a day. I heard many good things about it from people who stopped there. Passing Overmountain shelter, the Trail started up again and went up for an hour.

The big red barn kept getting smaller and smaller and soon was just a red dot.

I reached the top of Little Hump Mountain and could see small towns in the distance, roads that were shiny in the sunlight, and tiny tractors plowing the fields. From Little Hump I climbed to the top of Hump Mountain. All of it was above tree line with incredible 360 degree views. I found a comfortable place to sit down and enjoy the views. Endorphins were flowing freely in my system after the strenuous climb and I felt great!

I ended this memorable day at Apple House shelter at 6:00 pm. Four guys in their twenties and thirties were starting their dinners and doing camp chores. A young couple hiked in. They looked to be about twenty. She was Very attractive. She was fit, had curves in all the right places, and was bubbly and charming. Everyone was vying for her attention. They made their dinner and chatted with us. There was a chemistry between the couple that absolutely sizzled. We thought they were going to stay but the guy said: "Are you about ready to head out, Gina?" Gina said: "Sure!" And to us: "We like to tent by ourselves."

They only hiked about eight miles a day. That left a lot of energy..... At the rate they were going they would never make it to Katahdin before the snow. I don't think they cared.

As we watched Gina head down the Trail one of the guys summed it up best: "Lucky Bastard!"

I enjoyed a wide variety of hiking for the next seventy miles to the Virginia border. On the first day I hiked to the top of White Mountain. From there I crossed a rickety wooden bridge over a rapidly moving stream and then down a steep rocky pathway. A couple of times my hiking poles saved me from nasty falls. The pathway led to a beautiful waterfall. I followed a winding river and enjoyed watching the water flow by as I hiked in the shade of old oak trees. Some hikers were swimming in the river. It looked fun, but I just watched.

There was a very steep .3 mile climb to a shelter where I was going to spend the night. It was in an excellent location with views of the river and surrounding valley. When I read the shelter journal, entry after entry kept mentioning this big RAT! Forget it! I headed back down to the river. I was too far away to get to the next shelter so I started looking for a camping spot along the river. I found a great little spot in a shaded area within five feet of the water.

I put up my "tarp tent" for the first time. I cut off a piece of my bear bag rope, tied it between two trees, hung what was left of my tent over the rope, and staked down the sides. It looked pathetic with the duct tape covering the bear claw slashes. It was a clear night, so I didn't have to worry about rain. There was no netting so I put on a lot of Deet before getting into my sleeping bag. After dark the area came alive with fireflies. The last time I remember seeing fireflies was as a young child lying on my back in the front yard in Corpus Christi, Texas. This camping spot gave me good vibrations and the soothing sound of the river lulled me into a deep sleep.

A very steep climb of 2,000 feet in three miles greeted me the next morning. I passed a hiker that I would see again and again, all the way to Waynesboro, Virginia. His was an unusual hike. He was retired and in his late fifties. He was fulfilling his dream of thru-hiking the Appalachian Trail his own way. His wife would drop him off at a trailhead and drive to a predetermined location further along the Trail. When I saw her she would usually be sitting under a tree reading a book while she waited for her husband. They would spend the night at a motel and do the same thing over and over. They must have had a lot of money. That had to be expensive. Having your wife sharing your adventure, sleeping on a soft bed each night, eating at a restaurant each night, taking a shower each night, not having to carry a heavy backpack. (I'm not grumbling.)

In about four miles I came to Watauga Lake. I sat at a picnic table and enjoyed watching the activities. People were swimming in a roped off area. Families sat at picnic tables eating food that looked delicious to this skinny hiker. A man was giving kayak lessons to his girlfriend. Water skiers were shooting by behind loud motor boats. A tourist helicopter swooped down and hovered over the area. Heady stuff for a person used to the quiet of the forest.

The Trail followed the lake for half a mile and then headed steeply up to Watauga Dam. Another steep climb and I was at Vandeventer shelter for the night. There was a beautiful view of the lake. I could see the lights of towns along the lake. The neatly spaced rows of lights and being able to hear people talking in the marina far below, stand out in my memory.

There were three of us in the shelter that night. There was a talkative and friendly lady in her thirties who was trying to catch up to her hiking group and a guy in his early twenties. He was skinny even by hiker standards.

Hetalkedamileaminute.Neverstoppedtalking.Couldn'tstaystill.Nervous.Fi gety.HadafixationwithBears.Justaboutallhetalkedabout.

I wanted to grab him by the shoulders and say: "Take a deep breath. Now slooooowly exhale." There were only two people who carried weapons on the Trail that I know of. Fletch with his machete and this guy with his pistol. He lasted about another week on the Trail.

Two young hikers who were thru-hiking together, passed me as I was leaving Vandeventer shelter. Unique might be the diplomatic word to describe them. They would set mousetraps at all the shelters where they stayed and place the dead mice neatly in a row - sometimes ten or more. They were going to try to hike 41 miles to Damascus, Virginia this day. When I heard this I was thinking: "Are you crazy?!" And then: "Ah, to be young again." They made it, too. I saw them the next afternoon in Damascus.

4 DAMASCUS, VIRGINIA

Damascus, Virginia was only four miles from the Tennessee-Virginia state line. What a great way to be introduced to Virginia. Damascus had to be the most hiker friendly town on the Trail. It was a small town of probably five thousand people. Since 1987 it had hosted "Trail Days". I think I have the number right: In 2009, from May 15th - 17th, over 10,000 people participated in Trail Days. This was THE big thru-hiker event of the year. Wherever hikers were on the Trail, they stopped and hitchhiked to the event. People who had hiked the Trail (thru-hikers, section hikers, people who had hiked on the Trail) came back to reminisce. The town park was filled with tents. It was a non-stop party. There was a parade down the main street. Residents pelted the parade participants with water balloons and vice-versa. Hikers really did enjoy Trail Days and told about it to the end of their hikes. I missed it by about a week.

Damascus was the starting point of the Virginia Creeper Trail. This originally was a railroad trail built in the early 1900's to service the logging industry. The railroad pulled out many years ago and the trail was converted to a beautiful bike and hiking path. It was a popular tourist attraction and was jammed with bicyclists of all ages. Sometimes a family would pedal by. I liked seeing the pee-wee bikes of the little kids beside Mom and Dad's adult bikes. My hike followed the pathway along the river under shady elm trees and over wooden bridges made of thick logs.

Soon I left the pathway and headed up into the mountains. On the way up I saw a good sized bear. I stood completely still. The bear saw me and did the same. We stared at each other for quite a while. Finally the bear gave a low grumble and ran off. It's fun watching them run. Their front legs hit the ground together and then their back legs hit the ground together.

Their nose is practically touching the ground as they run. I spent the night at Saunders shelter. I had it all to myself for a change.

There were some good climbs the next day. It was chilly. I even had to put on my fleece pullover while climbing, which was unusual. I didn't see anyone while hiking that day. When I reached Thomas Knob Shelter it was cold and windy and started to rain. This was a good shelter. It was on the edge of a big bald which provided excellent views, and next to a tall pine forest on the edge of the bald. The shelter had two levels. I had the second level all to myself. I even had a window. The wind howled and the rain whipped against the window and I was glad to be inside.

My shelter-mates were a father and son just finishing a week long hike, and a guy from the Washington DC area who was into photography. Over the course of the hike I saw the bond that strengthened between father and son, father and daughter, mother and daughter, and mother and son. Hiking brought out the best in them. The father had promised his son a week long hike when he graduated from college. They both had an encyclopedic knowledge of anything having to do with hiking. I sure wasn't the authority with these two. I was the one asking the questions.

The storm raged through the night. By morning there was still a light rain coming down and it was chilly. Adam, the son, was curled up with his back against the back wall almost in a fetal position. His father peered out at the weather apprehensively. The man from DC was making his breakfast and didn't look exactly chipper. I ate my four Pop Tarts and was ready to go. I enjoyed hiking in the rain.

Outside the shelter acting like panhandlers waiting for a handout were a couple of feral ponies. I was in Grayson Highlands State Park, home of the wild ponies. This was an area of vast, grassy fields.

For much of the morning I was hiking in dense fog. About the only sound was of my hiking poles tapping the ground. All of a sudden three ponies appeared out of the fog. I was right next to them as they grazed. I could practically touch a beautiful dappled pony. They gave little snorts and kept on grazing. Since I wasn't bothering them, I stayed completely still. I was enveloped in fog. The only sound was of three wild ponies pulling up grass and chewing it. The sound was magnified in the stillness. It was so peaceful - a magical moment.

When the sun came out I saw at least forty ponies. Two ponies were frolicking and galloping together. It was amazing to see how fast and far they ran when not hampered by fences. I passed mothers nursing their foals and a protective stallion who snorted when I came too close to his family.

Virginia was by far the longest state to hike through – 537 miles. I was moving fast. My goal was to hike the Appalachian Trail in four months and be finished by early September at the latest. I started to use the shelter journals as a motivational tool beginning in Virginia. When I stopped at a shelter I would read the shelter journal and see who was ahead of me. I would see who was a day ahead, three days ahead, and a week ahead. It was fun catching up to the hikers and seeing them in person after reading their journals for a week or more. Some were easy to catch. Others I had to work at. Few had discipline when it came to staying on the Trail. I would close in on a group of hikers, get ready to meet them, but before I had the chance there would be a re-supply town and they were gone. They were sucked into the town "vortex" as they called it. There was so much to do in town. They could socialize with hikers they hadn't seen for a while, and meet new hikers. There were places to party, comfortable hostels, motels, and good restaurants. They would plan to stay a day and end up staying three days or more. It was easy to find an excuse, such as the threat of rain, and stay another day. For some, towns became a lot more fun than the Trail.

After an excellent day hiking through Grayson Highlands State Park and seeing the wild ponies, I ended up at Hurricane Mountain shelter. From Hurricane Mountain shelter I had a 27 mile day with lots of climbs and descents. I took a break at Partnership shelter. It had a shower, and there was even a phone 100 feet away where I could have ordered pizza and had it delivered. I was tempted to stay but it was only 4:00 pm.

When I walked up to the shelter I got a rude greeting from a yellow mongrel dog. Fortunately she was tied to a tree while her owner was taking a shower. Sometimes when a dog acts tough I can sense when it's not bluffing. I stayed away from this dog. A couple of hours later as I was climbing a steep trail at a pretty good clip I was passed by the dog and its owner. She was a tiny lady who probably weighed about 110 pounds. She passed me effortlessly. I was impressed. About fifteen minutes later I caught up with her as she was taking a break. Her name was Kell and her dog's name was Gracie. I tried hard to remember trail names as they were given to me. This one was easy: Grace Kelly. Kell was wary of strangers, just like her dog. She warned me that Gracie bites. I believed her. We hiked together for about twenty minutes. I had a feeling she was slowing her pace for me which was disconcerting. It was kind of a blow to my ego. She was interesting to talk to. The wall of suspicion began to evaporate. This killed me, but after a while I told her to go ahead because she was faster than me. (Just remember, I was nearing the end of a 27 mile day.) I know. I know. She was faster than me.

When I arrived at Chatfield shelter there was a party going on. The shelter was full. Kell got the last space. This was not good. The day had been drizzly and dark clouds were forming. I told the people in the shelter about my dilemma with the bear clawed tent. Most of the people in the shelter were section hikers just out for a few days. Nobody was budging. Kell, bless her heart, offered her space. I gratefully accepted. She put her tarp tent on the only space still left which was a tiny spot about ten feet downhill from the shelter. Tarp tents weigh only a couple of pounds. One of the drawbacks is that in heavy rain they have a tendency to leak. Guess what happened that night? In spades! A doozy of a thunderstorm came through at 1:00 am. I saw Kell's light go on and I felt terrible. I called down to her: "Kell. Are you O.K.? I can make room for you in the shelter." I heard a couple of grumbles. "I'm ok Wingo. Go back to sleep." The next morning Kell had puffy eyes and looked like the wrath of God. I felt even worse and apologized. She was nothing but kind. I should have gutted it out and put up my tarp tent without a fuss. I vowed that if a shelter was full in the future, I wouldn't ask for help. I just needed to make it to Waynesboro where I could buy a new tent.

Kell and Gracie. I didn't see her again but was glad to see that she summited by the end of September. The lady had a heart of gold!

The shelter was full because Bob was having a party. Bob started section hiking the Appalachian Trail in 1973. This evening was the completion of the entire Trail. It only took him thirty-six years to do it. Bob had invited twelve of his hiking friends to celebrate. One man flew in all the way from Paris. These were people he had hiked with over the years on different sections of the Trail. About half of the people were friends he had worked with over the years. They were celebrating at a picnic table and I was listening from the shelter. It was a lively group with lots of laughter. Everyone had a story. The booze was flowing heavily. The stories got livelier. Since many of them worked together, they started trying to top one another with "who had the lousiest boss" stories. At 10:30 they staggered off to bed.

From Chatfield shelter I hiked five miles to Highway 683 and three miles to Atkins, Virginia for a re-supply. I stopped at the Atkins Grocery and Deli. I devoured two very good BBQ sandwiches from the deli and had two large coffees with extra cream and sugar before I bought the groceries. I had to go to the only checkout counter in the store to pay for the BBQ and coffee. I stood there waiting to pay the cashier and stood there and stood there. The cashier finally acknowledged me and with a mischievous smile said: "Oh. You been waitin' long?" This was a quirky gentleman. As I was grocery shopping I would glance over and he was doing the same thing to other people. The guy had to be the store owner. No employee could get away with that for long. He also had the only grocery store in town.

A local resident gave me a ride back to the Trail. I was given a ride to or from town at least 40% of the time when I re-supplied on my thru-hike. Until I hit Maine I hardly even stuck my thumb out. Almost always I was picked up by locals or people who had been out hiking. Nice friendly people willing to give a ride to a dirty, smelly, scruffy hiker. There are a lot of good people who go out of their way to be kind.

Even with the re-supply I was able to hike nineteen miles. I could feel the effect of the BBQ sandwiches and it wasn't good. I reached Knot Maul Branch shelter and headed right to the privy. I had diarrhea for the next four days and felt worse with each passing day. The next two days were kind of a blur. I was worried that maybe it wasn't the BBQ and I might have picked up giardia from tainted water.

On the third afternoon I stopped at Jenny Knob shelter. I made a quick trip to the outhouse - if you could call it that. Since you are still reading this I need to warn you that I am not going to sugarcoat events that happened on my journey. You are going to get the good, the bad, and the ugly.

The outhouse was a wooden platform about 5 x 5 feet. Centered on the platform was a wooden box with a hole in it. A toilet seat was fastened to the box. There was absolutely no privacy. As you were sitting on the seat, you were looking at the back of the shelter which was twenty yards away. There were tents between you and the shelter. There was a long row of scout tents in front of the shelter. From your throne you were observing the activity of the people around the shelter. To even compound the indignity, the privy had been used so much it was ready to overflow. When I sat down on the toilet seat I was about three inches from touching.........You get the idea. The smell was awful!

At Jenny Knob shelter I encountered my first scout troop. It was the best one, too. All the tents were lined up in a neat line. The leaders were excellent. They enjoyed their kids and had good control but were not overbearing. The kids were young enough that they still wanted to interact with the adults. They were high energy; lots of noise, and lots of enthusiasm. They were all in bed by 9:30 pm and quiet after that. A violent thunderstorm came through in the night. Lightning strikes were hitting close by and frequently. It had my attention and I was in the shelter. The next morning the kids were enthusiastically telling their war stories. "You shoulda' seen the water in my tent!" "Well, you shoulda' seen the water in My tent! I got flooded!" It was true. They were clobbered by that thunderstorm. Their attitude was great! They had an adventure!

It took another day and a half to get to Pearisburg, Virginia. Food was hardly being digested. It was going right through me. I could feel myself getting weaker. I knew I had to do something. I got a room at the Holiday Lodge in Pearisburg, Virginia. I had a hot, soothing bath and took a refreshing nap. I needed to devise a plan to get rid of the diarrhea. I went to Hardees and bought the biggest hamburger on the menu - the Monster Burger. After that, I had a Mushroom Burger, two chocolate chip cookies, and a large coke. I wanted to put in some heavy, meaty food that was hard to digest. Darned if it didn't work! I was on the mend. I never had any more diarrhea for the rest of the trip.

I had an extra big re-supply at the Lion King in Pearisburg. I needed it because my appetite was absolutely voracious for the next few days. I talked on the phone with my sister, Johanna, and told her I would try to make it to her home in Afton, Virginia by the 14th of June. Johanna and her husband, Bob, live only four miles from the Appalachian Trail. I left Pearisburg on the 3rd of June. I had twelve days to hike 227 miles. I did it in eleven, averaging 20.6 miles a day. I pushed my body for eleven grueling days and could definitely feel the effort. It had been challenging and fun. I felt a sense of accomplishment.

I left Pearisburg at 11:00 am and entered the forest on the outskirts of town. There were wild strawberries along the pathway. They still had about two weeks to go to be ripe. It was a sunny day and I enjoyed the flow of the hike. I loved listening to the sounds of the forest - birds singing, trickling streams, rustling leaves, chipmunks scampering up trees, squirrels chattering at me as I walked through their territory.

I passed a hiker who had weather radar on his hand held computer. He said there was a big storm cell heading our way. I looked in the distance and sure enough he was right. The first rumblings started and soon I was in the middle of a big thunderstorm. I was still down in the trees and not on a ridge so I kept moving rapidly. I knew there was a shelter four miles up the Trail and I was moving as fast as I could to get there. The rain was pelting me. It was flowing in torrents off of the bill of my cap. I kept thinking: "It's got to be around the next corner." But it wasn't.

I caught up to two hikers. I knew I was close to the shelter so I didn't pass them. I didn't want to barge ahead of them and potentially take the last spot in the shelter. I finally saw the shelter. It was at the top of the mountain tucked into an area surrounded by trees. There was a turnoff to the shelter. The Trail continued on through open fields for another mile. There was still a lot of lightning in the area. The two hikers ahead of me kept going over that exposed area. Crazy! I headed to the shelter. There was only one space left. Whew!

It took a while to wind down. I was soaked! Rain jackets can only do so much. If you are in pounding rain for too long you are going to get wet. I changed into my camp clothes. I had gone six miles that day. At this rate I was never going to get to Johanna's by the 14th.

The storm raged for another hour. The people in the shelter were still excited about a lightning strike they had seen right next to the turnoff sign ten minutes earlier. They said that when the lightning hit the ground it buzzed like a high power voltage line. It was so powerful it shook the shelter. The thought immediately struck me: "What if I had passed the two hikers ahead of me?" Fortunately, it was only the thought that struck me.

These were five congenial hikers. Two were in their twenties, one in his thirties, another in his forties, and one in his late fifties. Two of them had thru-hiked the AT before. They were typical of many groups I saw on my hike – people of all ages interacting with mutual respect. No one in this group tried to dominate the conversation. They were cheerful, joking, and upbeat. Since I was the newcomer they were curious about me and I felt immediately included in the group.

In order to hike 20 mile days I started getting up between 5:30 am and 6:00 am. I worked out a system where I would get up, take my sleeping bag and air mattress and find a level spot far enough away from the shelter so that I wouldn't bother anyone. I would go back to the shelter and get my backpack. It took less than a minute and most of the time I didn't disturb anyone. I would deflate the air mattress, pack my backpack, and be on my way. This was the first part of June and the days were long. By the time I was ready to hike I could see the pathway. After hiking about fifteen minutes I would find a good spot to have my breakfast. If I was lucky, I would be enveloped in the first shafts of sunlight breaking through the trees.

I left the shelter at 6:00 am and put in eleven good hours of hiking – 25 miles. At 7:00 pm I arrived at my destination shelter and it was full. There were quite a few tents surrounding the shelter. The pickings for a decent spot were slim. I found a spot by a stream next to the pathway where people passed to get water. Since they had to wait for their water to be filtered, a couple of them asked about my tent. I explained about the claw marks and told the bear story. Later I could hear the story being repeated at the shelter. A young group of "intellectuals" had the shelter. They had gotten there before 2:00 pm after a rugged seven mile day. There were four men and four women. They sat around the campfire smoking cigarettes and writing in their personal journals. They surrounded the campfire and didn't interact with any of the other hikers. Very superior. As I was in my sleeping bag I heard one of them say: "Maybe a bear will finish him off tonight."

It rained all the next day and I worked hard to get in 18 miles. It was dark when I arrived at the shelter. It was raining heavily and the shelter was full. Throughout my hike, if I arrived late to a shelter and it was raining, the shelter was full. People who normally camped wanted to spend the night in a shelter if it was raining. A lot of people would hold their shelter space day after day until the rain stopped. Talk about grouchy, negative people. Those were extremely depressing places that I avoided like the plague.

I had to put up my tarp tent in the rain and hope for the best. Before doing this, I stopped at the shelter to get out of the rain for a few minutes and steel myself for the ordeal ahead. Headlamps were softly glowing; their lights bobbing around the interior of the shelter. People were talking in soft murmurs. There was warmth generated by warm bodies in a partially enclosed area. It almost seemed cozy until I noticed how many people were in the shelter. This shelter was designed to hold eight people and there had to have been twelve of them packed in like sardines.

I started looking for a level spot to put my tent. It was difficult to do. I had no depth perception in the dark. I didn't have a headlamp yet, so I used the little flashlight my brother, Doug, gave me for Christmas. It didn't need disposable batteries and I had to wind it up to keep the light strong. It made a whirring sound when I was winding it. I spent the next half hour in the steady rain, whirring the flashlight, and positioning it so that I could set up the tent.

I attached a rope between two trees, put the tarp over the rope, and staked the sides of the tarp into the ground. I couldn't tell if the area was flat or not. It wasn't. The water slid down from the uphill side of my tent and rolled onto my ground cloth inside the tent. The ends of the tent were open and I was getting sprayed by rain so I put my raincoat over the end where my head was going to be. It helped a little.

I got into my sleeping bag. "Sniff… Sniff… What's that smell?" Next to my head, at the base of the tree, someone had taken a dump and partially covered it. Now the rain had opened it up.

Could it get any worse? Of course! The rain started to drip, drip, drip, through the bear claw patchwork and was steadily soaking my sleeping bag. Groan.

It rained all night. My sleeping bag was wet and cold. I was miserable. Somehow I managed about four hours of sleep. I packed up as best I could the next morning. Everything was wet and it made my pack heavy. My mood should have been rotten but it wasn't. This day turned into an unexpectedly fun day although the end of it was kind of weird.

I would start hiking each day at a slow pace to gradually warm up the muscles. After an hour I would be in the groove. Early in my hike I was passed by Cargen and Katz. They had both recently graduated from Georgia Tech. They had been roommates since their freshman year in college. They needed to do a fast thru-hike because both had been accepted to graduate school. When they passed me they gave me kind of an indifferent nod, just like I did when I passed other hikers. We were on a long steep grade that would continue for another couple of hours. My body kicked into Go Mode. They were both hiking fast and it took an hour to catch them. As I passed they both asked: "Who are you?" I hiked and chatted with them for two more hours. Finally, they took a break and I kept going. I passed the Audie Murphy Monument. This was where Audie Murphy died in a plane crash. It was a beautiful area and a fitting tribute to a brave soldier.

In the afternoon I reached Dragon's Tooth. I had been hearing good things about it since I started hiking the Trail. There was a steep climb to the top of Cove Mountain. On the side of the mountain was a rocky area with huge jagged boulders. There was a lot of hand over hand descending with some steep drop offs. It was challenging and fun.

After Dragon's Tooth I continued another nine miles and reached Johns

Spring shelter by 8:00 pm. I had hiked over twenty difficult miles and was ready to call it a day. The shelter was only a mile from a college town and it was a Saturday night. There were ten thru-hikers who greeted me - six men and four women. It was almost dark and everyone was congregated around a lively campfire. On the picnic table were two cases of Bud Lite. The first case was nearly empty. There were hot dogs and buns and all the fixings. The leader of the group greeted me and told me they were waiting for their college friends who were bringing more beer: "And then we are Really going to party!" It looked like they were doing just fine on their own. They offered me a beer. They were in a good mood. A very good mood. All four of the women were in their twenties and good looking. One of them was a professional belly dancer. She started swaying sensuously. The noise level grew louder and the language more vulgar. The man who seemed to be manipulating this activity got behind his girlfriend and wrapped his arms around her. She bent over and he began to slowly caress her butt; then even more slowly he started to slide his hand.......I said to myself: "I'm outta' here!"

I quietly moved away from the picnic table, grabbed my backpack, and headed back to the Trail. Nobody even noticed I was gone. Fortunately, Catawba Mountain shelter was only a mile away. The path was wet and slippery. It was full of rocks of all sizes. I was navigating without my flashlight because I needed my hands for my hiking poles. I saw the light from a headlamp approaching from behind. It was Cargen and Katz. They had heard the noise from the partiers and kept right on going. They put me in the middle. Cargen was leading and Katz was behind me shining his headlamp beam at my feet as we headed to the shelter. It was 10:00 pm when arrived. Cargen peered into the shelter with his headlamp. There was one man at the shelter who was asleep. He was startled and yelled: "AAAAHHHH!" He must have thought it was a bear. Cargen apologized profusely. The guy grumbled and didn't say anything more.

Cargen and Katz found a place to put their tent. I stayed in the shelter. I had hiked 25 miles that day including some very strenuous hiking. As quietly as I could I got ready for bed and into my sleeping bag. My body had worked so hard it wasn't ready to come down. I couldn't stay still. I kept shifting back and forth in my sleeping bag. My legs would convulsively kick. After a half hour of this the guy said loudly: "Are You About Ready To Stop Making Noise?" It startled me. Those are the only words he had said to me.

"Sure. Sorry."

About five minutes later he let out a gigantic fart. If that wasn't a statement of discontent I don't know what was. I woke up at 5:30 the next morning. That thrilled him, too. I was gone by 6:00 am. My destination was McAfee Knob. I wanted to be there early in the morning.

5 MCAFEE KNOB

McAfee Knob was one of the most popular places on the Appalachian Trail. It was a slab of rock jutting out from the mountain with a long sheer drop off. I had seen pictures of hikers with their legs dangling over McAfee Knob. I wondered if I would be able to sit on the knob with my legs hanging over the side. This was the moment of truth.............! It was anti climatic. I walked out to the edge and sat down with my legs dangling over the side and enjoyed the view. What a great place! I can see why it was so popular. It was quiet and peaceful. I could hear the occasional moooo of cattle in the valley far below. The sun was just starting to make an appearance and I was sitting majestically on McAfee Knob, my senses absorbing all the beauty around me. Wingo! King of the Mountain!

I was soon joined by Posiedon who I would hike with the rest of the day. I took his picture from the side showing him with his feet hanging over the edge. This was another excellent hiking day. There were some really tough climbs and descents with few letups. Posiedon was in his early thirties. My strength was long, steep climbs. I could hold my own with just about anyone. On climbs, this guy stayed right on my heels and I could tell he was hurting less than I was. Nice guy. I kept track of him in the shelter journals. It took him less than four months to hike the Trail.

We stopped for a break on Tinker Ridge. There were awesome views. Posiedon took out his map and pointed to a mountain way in the distance: "That's McAfee Mountain." I couldn't believe it. We had been there just hours earlier. It looked days away to me.

At 3:00 pm we came out of the mountains and hit Highway 220. A quarter mile to the west was a big grocery store. I said so long to Posiedon and headed over to re-supply.

I was back on the Trail by 4:30 pm and continued another five miles to Fullhart Knob shelter. That was a productive day - 23 miles with a re-supply. I had the shelter to myself. There were two other people but they were tenting. This shelter was on top of a mountain and angled so I had a view of a star filled sky from my sleeping bag. I woke up a couple of times in the night and enjoyed gazing at the stars before going back to sleep. The only water source was rainwater that rolled off of the roof into a collection barrel. I passed on drinking it although I was getting low.

After 250 miles of hiking in Virginia some of the entries in the shelter journals were getting negative. They kept mentioning that hiking in Virginia was like hiking through a long green tunnel - nothing but pathway and trees. Boring, boring, boring.

This was when I first started seeing the "stare". I would come into a shelter after a long day of hiking and see that some of the people were genuinely tired. They had no energy. When they moved they groaned. They hobbled listlessly around the shelter. They didn't want to talk to anyone. They had a tired, defeated look. They sat motionless and stared straight ahead. This hike had turned out to be more than they had bargained for and they were beginning to realize it. Many people dropped out in Virginia.

Virginia was hardly a "long green tunnel". Nothing could be further from the truth. The state had an amazing variety of beauty. There were healthy forests with vibrant colors. I think it was the most colorful state that I hiked through. The rhododendrons first started to bloom while I was in Virginia. Huge areas were covered with rhododendron. The colors made me stop and soak in their beauty. There were white flowers with delicate pink interiors, light purple flowers, and pink flowers with black lined geometrical patterns on the inside. I have always enjoyed bright colors and walking through forests full of blooming rhododendron was a treat.

There was lush undergrowth. Since there had been plenty of rain, the undergrowth was sometimes quite thick. That posed a problem when I approached a rattlesnake on the Trail in Central Virginia. It was a big long one. Fortunately it wasn't coiled. It just stared at me and didn't move. I didn't want to move it with my hiking poles and the Trail was too narrow to maneuver around it, so I decided to get off of the Trail and go around it. As I was pushing my way through thick, thorny, brush, I tripped on a fallen branch, fell backwards and was on my back staring at the snake from about snake eye level. It continued to stare at me and flick its tongue. With some effort I was able to get upright, brush myself off with what dignity I had left, and continue on my way. Mr. Cool.

Virginia was teeming with wildlife. I saw more deer, bear, raccoon, skunk, snakes, and wild turkey than in any other state. The forests were alive with birds; their songs crystal clear. The wild ponies of the Graceland Highlands, Virginia Creeper Trail, Dragon's Tooth, Tinker Cliffs, and

McAfee Knob, just to name a few, and hikers were whining about the "long green tunnel?"

Hiking the actual Trail in Virginia was fun. Whoever created the hiking routes had an eye for beauty and a love of hiking. If there was a waterfall, pond, swamp, stream, or anything out of the ordinary, the Trail would pass by it. If I saw a mountain ahead, I knew without a doubt, I would be on top of it eventually. Some days the Trail would be mellow and gentle. Sometimes it followed old mountain roads - old, old mountain roads probably dating back a couple of hundred years with some of the original rockwork. Other days the Trail went practically straight up, which burned my legs, left me gasping for breath, and soaked my shirt with sweat. Occasionally the Trail would go around the side of a mountain and I enjoyed the views of towns and fields in the valleys below. I was always stumbling on rocks and roots as I was gazing at the sights below. My hiking poles saved my butt many times. There were rock days where most of the day was spent hiking over all different sizes and shapes of rocks. I had to hop from rock to rock, hoping that when I landed, the rock didn't wobble. Those were mentally tiring days. I had to stay focused the whole time or risk a broken leg or sprained ankle.

Over and over the Trail creators would take us to mountains with big overhanging rock formations at the top. The views were spectacular, but hiking over big slabs of rock with precarious footing and the potential to slide over the side was scary. When it was raining or after a rain it was very scary. I had my first fall on these slick rocks. I hit my knee hard and bloodied it. I was fortunate not to have slipped off of the side. The knee ached for two months and I kept accidentally hitting it with my hiking poles which didn't help.

I finally made it to a shelter after spending hours trying not to kill myself on the rock slabs. Ten by Ten came in a few minutes later. His leg and elbow were bleeding. "Did you hear me yelling out there, Wingo? That scared the shit out of me!" Those big overhanging rock slabs were dangerous, yet time after time, the Trail creators would route us over them. I wanted to say: "Enough already! Yes! Beautiful views! I don't want to see any more of them!"

From Fulhardt Knob shelter to Bobblets Gap shelter I only hiked 13 miles. By the time I was close to Bobblets Gap the skies were getting dark and it looked like a thunderstorm was moving in. There was a lightning strike close by and a loud Boom and I headed to the shelter. It was only 4:00 pm. I was the first to arrive. Within an hour the shelter was full. I was disgusted with myself. The thunderstorm didn't materialize. I pretty much wimped out. This shelter had a spring with pure, cold delicious water. The hikers at the shelter were people I hadn't met yet. Most were in their twenties.

I heard on a couple of occasions of a hiker killing a grouse. Getting charged by a grouse protecting its young was something that happened occasionally. Just before Damascus, Virginia I had been charged by a really aggressive grouse. Her nest was only ten feet from the Trail. She displayed her feathers like a peacock, made angry noises, and headed straight toward me. I kept moving to get out of her territory. When she came too close, I turned around, clicked my hiking poles at her and said: "Hey. Hey." She backed away. I kept moving thinking that was the end of it and she charged me again. I finally made it out of her area. The grouse is a beautiful bird. I always thought they were a drab brown. Almost every hiker sooner or later was charged by a grouse.

One of the hikers said: "Hey. You're the guy who killed the grouse, aren't you?" Grouse killer had a pleased smile on his face like he thought he was a celebrity. "Guilty. Chuckle. Chuckle." He had been charged by a grouse protecting her young. He then beat her to death with his hiking pole, carried her to the next shelter and ate her for dinner. Unless the other parent was around to take care of the young chicks, they starved to death.

Senseless killing bothered me on the Trail. I saw a rattlesnake with its head chopped off. I saw a couple of blacksnakes that were cut in two. Sure they are big and look menacing, but they are harmless and do a wonderful job of getting rid of mice. There was a shelter journal entry at one of the shelters that read: "There is a bull snake at this shelter. DON'T KILL IT!" Why some people get enjoyment in taking life is beyond my understanding.

The next day I hiked 24 miles from Bobblets Gap to Thunder Hill shelter. At the end of the day I went through the "Guillotine." Perched between two big boulders was a rock right above my head that had probably been there for millions of years. I passed rapidly under it: "Just in case."

From Thunder Hill shelter to Punchbowl shelter where I spent the night, I hiked 25 miles. One of the mountains I passed was Bluff Mountain. Near the top of Bluff Mountain I came across a worn stone marker. The marker was quite old. It marked the spot where the little body of a child named Ottie was found curled up like he had gone to sleep and never awakened. My Thru-Hikers' Companion Guidebook gave more details. Since I lost that page, this is going to be from memory. In 1890, five year old Ottie wandered away from his school playground. The townspeople searched for him for days. The following spring they found his little body way at the top of Bluff Mountain. It was six miles from the schoolyard. To me it was touching. When he died he was one year older than my grandmother. She was born in 1886. She lived a long, good life. Poor Ottie!

This was the first time the Trail met the Blueridge Parkway. Hiking close to the Blueridge Parkway was always disconcerting. I would think I was deep in the woods and a car would whiz by. Punchbowl shelter was near the Blueridge Parkway. Just before I arrived at the shelter I met a man in his sixties wearing a day pack:

"Would you like some trail magic?"

"Sure."

"Let me go back to my truck and I will meet you at the shelter in ten minutes."

"Great!"

Ten minutes later he rolled in a cart that had a Coleman camp stove and an ice chest. He pulled a big container of orange juice out of the ice chest.

"Help yourself."

"Thanks."

"How would you like your eggs?"

"Over easy?"

He cooked me three eggs, Kielbasa sausage which was wonderful, and six pancakes.

"There's plenty more if you want it."

"No. No. Thanks a lot."

John's son had hiked the Appalachian Trail a couple of years before. John gave trail magic to his son and trail friends and just kept doing it. He was just a real nice guy. I enjoyed talking with him. There was another shelter he was heading to, so we said good-bye. I had put in a 25 mile day and that good food hit the spot. About fifteen minutes after John left, three more hikers arrived at the shelter. It was probably cruel but I told about my trail magic. It was cruel. They stared glumly at their Ramen noodles that night.

After a while boots and socks smell awful! Everyone puts them outside the shelter at night so they don't have to smell them. They are next to your head, but outside the shelter. If you need to get up in the night, you can get out of your sleeping bag, swivel around, hang your legs over the shelter floor, and put your feet into the boots. This night there were four people at the shelter: Y-Knot, Pyrofly, his girlfriend Lucky Star, and Wingo. We all had our boots, socks, and crocks lined up outside the shelter when we went to bed. At 6:00 am I was the first to wake up. I very quietly, so as not to disturb anyone, swiveled over the edge of the shelter and looked down to find my boots and socks to put them on. My socks weren't there. I looked underneath the shelter. I looked around all the boots and crocks. They weren't there. They had such a powerful odor they couldn't be in my pack. I had worn out socks rapidly and they were the only pair I had left. I needed them! I woke up Pyrofly and Lucky Star. "Have you seen my socks?" They looked through their things. Lucky Star noticed that one of her crocs was missing. By now Y-Knot was awake. His crocs were missing. He started roving around the shelter grounds looking for them. He found Lucky Star's croc, but not his own. There were little raccoon tracks around the area.

Great! No socks. I would have to hike to the nearest road, hitchhike to the nearest town, and buy some socks. My feet would have been hamburger meat by then.

Pyrofly said: "Wingo, I have four pair of socks in my pack. You can have a pair of mine." I gratefully accepted. They were clean. They even smelled good. That was very generous.

After leaving Punchbowl shelter I leapfrogged for a good part of the day with Pyrofly and Lucky Star. They caught up to me while I was taking a break under big shady oak trees next to a stream. It was a hot day. There was a deep pool in the stream and hikers were immersed in the water. That was too inviting for Pyrofly and Lucky Star. It was the last time I saw them.

I planned on catching up to them after taking a five day break at my sisters. I was going to return the socks to Pyrofly with a $20 bill inside to enjoy at an all-you-can-eat restaurant. I washed those socks three times to get the odor out. From reading shelter journals I knew I was closing in on Pyrofly and Lucky Star in the Shenandoahs, but they must have taken a town stop and I passed them. I knew they liked their beer. In Duncannon, Pennsylvania there is a legendary hotel called the Doyle where all thru-hikers stop for a beer. I talked to the owner of the Doyle who said he would put the socks with the re-supply boxes. Pyrofly should have reached the Doyle within five days of when I was there. I never did find out if the socks made it back to him. I hope so. He went out of his way to help me and I did appreciate it.

I put in eleven good hours of hiking and reached my destination by 6:00 pm. There were lots of people tenting around the shelter but only three section hikers sharing the shelter with me. The section hikers lived for hiking and were fun to talk to. One was sixty-five, another was sixty-two, and the third was in his fifties. They had been section hiking together for years.

This was the first time I met Blackbird and One Step. Blackbird carried a sixty pound pack. His food bag alone weighed more than my fully loaded pack. He showed me his grocery receipt and it was about two feet long. At a Dollar General store I could completely re-supply with five days of food for between thirty-five and forty dollars. His receipt was $110. He was a slow hiker. Everyone passed him. Pans banged around in his backpack as he hiked. He took few days off; hardly ever stayed at a motel or hostel. He just kept plodding on - month after month. He was the tortoise to all of the hares. He stayed ahead of them, too. He summited Katahdin in late September.

One Step was a class act on the Trail. He was easy going, helpful, inquisitive, positive. He was impressed with how many miles I had covered since I started. He said loudly: "You started April 28th? Wow!" He asked how many miles I hiked in a day. I told him that for the last few days I had been averaging 22 miles a day. "Wow!" We were sitting around a picnic table making our dinner with four other hikers. He asked how light my backpack was. I was low on food and I told him less than 20#. I told him it normally weighed 25# to 28# with food and water. Everyone at the table started to listen. We had a discussion on lightweight backpacking. Everyone participated and it was a lively, entertaining discussion. Even the three section hikers were listening intently from the shelter.

That was one of One Step's qualities. He could get a good discussion going. He was probably in his early thirties, although I could be way off. He could be younger or older. His language was that of the younger crowd. He fit in easily with that group. He got along well with everyone. I never did find out what he did for a living. If he wasn't a guidance councilor to kids or adults, he should have been.

That night a powerful thunderstorm came through. I was glad to be in the shelter. Early the next morning when I unzipped my sleeping bag, the three section hikers unzipped theirs almost simultaneously. It was like they were waiting for me to get up but didn't want to disturb me until I did. They wanted to talk and we did. They had been listening to the conversation from the night before. Their daily mileage was about eight miles. They were so deferential to me it was almost embarrassing. Just before I left one of them said: "Wingo. You go kick those young kid's butts, today!" I assured him I would.

Two hours into the hike I ran into some excellent trail magic. I was starting to run low on food so the timing was perfect. A couple in their late fifties had been providing trail magic for the last twenty years at the spot where I was standing. They drove their trailer from Texas, set up their big umbrella, and fed hikers for five days. They had a log book for every year with the picture, trail name, and a written message from each hiker. They eagerly showed me the log books. They were marking their 28th wedding anniversary and had met at the next shelter down the Trail. It was 8:00 am and I was the only hiker there. They said: "Eat as much as you want." (That was music to my ears!) They didn't even blink when I started putting away the food. In twenty years they had probably seen some impressive eating. I had six pancakes with butter and syrup, four pieces of bacon, scrambled eggs, cookies, four pieces of bread with peanut butter and jelly, a banana, grapes, an apple, potato chips, two cokes, and a wonderful cup of coffee with cream and sugar. They enjoyed watching my delight as I put away the delicious food.

I was glad to be tanked up with food because this was a monster of a hiking day. I didn't know it was coming. Wow! What a day. It seemed like I was climbing for hours. I passed at least twelve young thru-hikers that day. I hadn't seen any of them before and didn't see any of them again. Young partiers. They were usually taking a break when I passed them; smoking their cigarettes, and talking with gravelly voices. Four of them were asleep on a big slab of rock right on the Trail. It must have been a rough night.

I was hiking at my top speed and was passed by a tall, wiry guy. For the next two hours we went non-stop. I would pass him. He would pass me. Just before reaching the top, I pulled a little bit ahead. When I finally reached the top I found a good place with a view to rest. Since there were streams around I didn't hold back on drinking my water. It was early June and a hot day. I chugged my first 32 ounce container and finished half of my next container before he showed up. He was panting pretty hard just like I was when I arrived. The first thing he did was open a pack of cigarettes and light one up. Talk about addiction. After he finished his cigarette, he drank some water. He didn't have an ounce of fat on him. About a week later he started passing blood in his urine and feces. His body was feeding off of its muscle. He never got a hiker appetite. Never could eat a lot of food. He unfortunately had to leave the Trail.

I put in over a twenty mile day in those high mountains and by the time I arrived at the next shelter I was pooped. The shelter was beside a little pond and people were fishing. It was a pretty setting with tall pines and grassy areas. There were a lot of people tenting. I came in late and fortunately there was one shelter space left. This was a congenial group. The man who dominated the conversation was retired, in his late fifties, and had a long white beard. His trail name was Robo. The man had the gift of gab. He was intelligent, opinionated, and very entertaining.

I met Birdie and Bubbles for the first time. I would see them again and again all the way into New Hampshire. They were a couple in their mid-twenties. I loved listening to them talk. I always wondered who their role models were: "What would you like for dinner, darling?" "I'll let you decide, dearest."

That night was a terrible night for no-see-ums in the shelter. These are tiny bugs that if you don't stay covered will bite the heck out of you. I still had my 20 degree bag in June and I could only keep it closed for so long. When I opened it up I would start to itch all over. I was squirming in that bag all night long. Everyone in the shelter was. What an awful night! I only slept a couple of hours. I couldn't take it any longer and left the next morning at 4:30. I was on the Trail in the dark. Within a half an hour it was starting to get light enough to put away the flashlight. I saw a beautiful sunrise as I was eating my Pop Tarts. This was a hard day of hiking on a rocky Trail.

The running shoes I had started my hike with were shot. My left shoe was ripped so badly that part of my sock was hanging out. When a rock would hit that area the pain was excruciating. That was THE dumbest mistake I made on the whole hike - waiting 853 miles before replacing shoes that should have been replaced at 500 miles. By the time I reached my sister's house the bottoms of my feet were puffed and stayed that way for the rest of the hike.

Two days of hard hiking and little sleep and I was starting to feel it. I was glad to get to the shelter that night. One Step was at the shelter and had my fanny pack which I had forgotten to take with me a couple of days earlier. There was a hiker feed in Waynesboro at 5:00 pm the next day. He needed to hike twenty-three miles to get there. He set his alarm for 3:30 am. Aggressive mice kept most of us up during the night. You could hear them drilling into the packs with their feet. It made a buzzing sound like a dragonfly. When One Step's alarm went off he got up and packed. Just before he left he said quietly and with a smile: "Good-bye old dude."

I couldn't sleep so I decided to hit the Trail early. I was out of food. Two miles past the shelter was a road that headed steeply downhill for two miles to a store. It was just opening when I arrived. I re-supplied and had a wonderful cup of coffee which I desperately needed. I trudged back up the steep, steep hill. The only vehicles to pass me were in four wheel drive. I just had eight more hours of hiking to go and I would be able to take a badly needed break at my sisters. I couldn't wait.

Between Pearisburg and Waynesboro the calorie burn was incredible. I was hiking with a twenty-eight pound pack in mountains with steep climbs and descents and I was hiking fast. I would guess I was burning 500 calories an hour. I was hiking twelve hours a day. That's about 6,000 calories a day. I was putting over 5,000 calories into my body each day and losing an alarming amount of weight.

I began counting down the miles and hours on the last day. When I was within eight miles of Rockfish Gap I started hiking through an area I had day hiked while visiting my sister. It was fun seeing familiar places and anticipating what was coming next. "There should be a stone wall in about a mile. Yep. There it is." "There's a steep downhill, then I cross a stream, and there's a shelter just on the other side. Yep. There it is."

I made it to Rockfish Gap at 5:00 pm. I called my sister. Bob answered the phone. He sounded surprised: "I didn't think you were going to be here until tomorrow."

Bob picked me up at Rockfish Gap. It was great seeing him. It felt good sitting on the soft seat of the truck. I relaxed and enjoyed the ride. Bob quietly opened his window to get a flow of fresh air circulating through the truck. I asked: "That bad, Huh?" "Yep." It was great seeing Johanna! When I entered the house I was immediately hit with the aroma of roasting lamb. It is one of my all-time favorite smells. Johanna and Bob had invited some of their tennis friends for dinner. Was my timing perfect of what? I was an uninvited guest but I enjoyed it. I met some very interesting people and even got to tell my bear story.

I had a shower at Standing Bear Hostel when I finished the Smokies, a shower at Elmer's Sunnybank Hostel in Hot Springs, North Carolina, and a bath at the Holiday Lodge in Pearisburg, Virginia. That was it. I took a nice, hot, relaxing bath. It felt great! When I finished the bathwater was a dirty yellow and I was squeaky clean,

Johanna and Bob were startled to see how thin I was. When I started my thru-hike I weighed 132 pounds. I now weighed 123. I could practically read Johanna's mind. "No. This won't do. I've got to get some weight back on Jim." Boy, did I eat well on my visit - wonderful meals and continuous grazing in between. By the time I was ready to head back to the Trail I was back to 132 pounds. This was a time of sleeping late on a soft comfortable bed, enjoying good conversations with Johanna and Bob, and resting.

I drove to the outfitters in Waynesboro and bought some new hiking shoes, a Pocket Rocket stove, a little blanket liner which replaced my 20 degree sleeping bag, (bad idea), and a Big Agnes Seedhouse SL1 tent that I loved.

Johanna and Bob left for a tennis tournament and I spent two more days at their house. I only meant to spend one. I had the pack on my back and walked to the end of the driveway and it started to sprinkle. It wasn't difficult to talk myself into one more day of rest. I even took a luxury bubble bath complete with jets to sooth tight muscles.

6 THE SHENANDOAHS

Every thru-hiker looked forward to hiking in the Shenandoahs. It had waysides where you could buy hamburgers and sodas. The famed blackberry shake was a hiker favorite. The Shenandoah National Park had a well-deserved reputation of being a beautiful park with healthy forests and a variety of animals. It had well maintained trails with easy hiking. Hikers in decent shape expected to average over twenty miles a day and cross the 107 miles of the Shenandoah National Park in five days.

I bought at least twenty pounds of food and when I hiked the four miles uphill from my sister's house back to the Trail my pack weighed over forty pounds. Rookie! Rookie! Rookie! I was huffing and puffing. I didn't have to re-supply again until I was in West Virginia.

The extra pack weight was hurting my shoulders. My thighs were screaming with pain on the down-hills. The thigh pain lasted a day. My body had to gradually work back into the hike. It was four days before I hit my stride again.

The first day back on the Trail I overdid it. I hiked 19 miles with the extra heavy pack and that didn't include the mileage from my sister's to the trailhead. That evening my heart rate was way up and didn't come down for a long time. Even the next morning it was elevated. I was trying to make it to Blackrock Hut but ran out of daylight. I ended up about a mile short. I used my new headlamp that my sister gave me. It worked great. I found a level camping spot and put up my new tent for the first time. Setting up the tent was easy. I hung my bear bag, had dinner, brushed my teeth, and got into my sleeping blanket. I was so tired, I couldn't sleep. Soon I started to hear branches snapping. This was about the first time I had been tenting alone since my bear encounter. The noises could not be ignored. Something was out there and I knew I had to meet it head on. I put my shoes on, unzipped the tent, and got out. Three deer were browsing nearby. Whew! Grazing in this spot was part of their nightly routine and they were sharing it with me. Back in my sleeping blanket, I enjoyed listening to them munch on the grass in the stillness of the night.

I was taking a break at Blackrock Hut (Shelters were called huts in the Shenandoahs.) when I met Yard Sale, Jim Dandy, and Bee Man. I hiked with them for three days. Sometimes we would hike together and talk. Mostly we would hike alone and finish the day at the same shelter. I enjoyed their company. They even wanted me to be part of their group. Although they were pushing their bodies to the limit and were totally exhausted at the end of the day, they still exuded a positive energy.

Yard Sale had two grown daughters in their twenties. My guess is that she was in her early fifties. She had a body that a twenty-five year old would be proud of. She had completed 23 marathons and a few triathlons. She was a good conversationalist and interesting lady. When she started her thru-hike she weighed 131 pounds. She was now 110 pounds. She looked great, but she didn't have any fat reserves. I don't think she knew how to eat enough to compensate for calorie burn. While I was around her I could see how not being able to stop her weight loss was worrying her. I was sad to hear that she ended her thru-hike at Harpers Ferry, West Virginia. For her own health it was the right thing to do.

Jim Dandy was in his late fifties. He had already lost forty pounds and probably had twenty more to go. He had a burning desire to complete his thru-hike. He had already lost toenails and banged himself badly on falls on rocks. He would come into the hut at the end of the day just groaning with exhaustion. I could tell he was proud of himself. He could now do consecutive eighteen mile days. He fell while hiking on the rocks in Pennsylvania and broke his nose. He went to the doctor, had it set, and was back on the Trail the next day. The guy was tough as nails. He made it to Katahdin in early October. I was glad for him. No one wanted it more.

Bee Man was in his thirties. He was easygoing and happy to be part of the group. He would groan with Yard Sale and Jim Dandy at the end of the day, but I don't think he was hurting nearly as much as they were. He summited Katahdin on the 11th of October.

We did a lot of talking. The topics ranged all over the place. They all had a good sense of humor and could give you the needle, too. I made my first navigational error with this group. There were little trails down to shelters. They were usually only one or two tenths of a mile long. We were taking a break at one of the huts and I took off ahead of the group. I headed up the little trail from the hut back to the AT. When I reached the Trail, I turned south instead of north. (It's easy to do if you are not paying attention.) I hiked a couple of miles before I came to a trailhead next to a road. I saw a car in the trailhead parking lot that looked familiar. Oh No! I turned around and rapidly started retracing my steps; most of it uphill in the June heat. I was trying to get past the entrance to the hut before Yard Sale, Jim Dandy, and Bee Man finished taking their break. I passed the entrance to the hut. I didn't see them. Maybe they were still taking a break. I saw Yard Sale up ahead. Shit! I'm not going to hear the end of this.

"Wingo! I thought you were ahead of us. Hey, Jim Dandy. Look. It's Wingo."

Jim Dandy was enjoying this: "Bee Man. Look who's behind us. It's Wingo! What happened Wingo?"

"I don't want to talk about it."

"Wingo Went South Instead Of North!"

"Way to go Wingo!"

Later as I was hiking with Jim Dandy he said confidentially: "I've done the same thing, Wingo."

This was a beautiful area. There was an abundance of deer. They had no fear of hikers. You could walk right by them and they would look up, stare at you for a couple of seconds, and continue grazing. Close to picnic areas I saw too many bears. One bear was obviously used to being fed. It was a big one. It was ahead of me on the pathway. I headed toward it clicking my hiking poles together. It didn't move. I continued moving ahead. It was starting to get too close for comfort. I clicked louder. "Get out of here! Go! GO!" The bear reluctantly left the pathway, hopped onto a log, and balanced on it. It looked cute, pouting on the fallen tree.

A couple of days later I stopped for the night at Pass Mountain hut at 4:00 pm. About a quarter mile before I reached the hut I saw a bear. When I mentioned it to the five people who were already there, they had all seen it. Their attitude was like: "So what." That's how many bears there were in the Shenandoahs.

At Pass Mountain hut I encountered the absolute worst youth group. There were fourteen kids between twelve and seventeen with two leaders. One of the leaders was in his early thirties. The main leader was in his fifties. The younger leader, ferret face, was the first to arrive at 4:00 pm. There was absolutely no organization. Kids kept coming in for the next five hours. There were ten other thru-hikers tenting and using the hut. It was as if we didn't exist. These kids were loud, obnoxious, and crude. Whenever a hiker in their group neared the hut, he would cry: HI! HO!, HI! HO! All the hikers would echo at the top of their lungs: HI! HO!, HI! HO!, HI! HO!, HI! HO! This kept going into the night. What a bunch of goofballs!

They didn't have a strong hiker with the stragglers. At 9:00 pm the last straggler had not made it to the hut. There was a debate among the leaders about who was going to look for him. Nobody wanted to look for him. It was like: "You go." "No. I don't want to go. You go." Finally a couple of them grudgingly went out searching for the lost hiker. Kids who had hiked with him earlier in the day said he had complained about running out of energy. For the next half hour you could hear them yelling his name. They came back at 10:00 pm. They couldn't find him. The leader then called a Forest Ranger who started a search. The poor little guy must have been frightened out of his wits. Lost and in the dark, he probably jumped every time he heard a twig snap. At 2:00 am a none too pleased Forest Ranger arrived at the hut with the missing child.

Earlier, at 5:00 pm, I was making my dinner at the hut. I was sitting at the picnic table with a lady in her fifties who was section hiking and ferret face. A snake about as thin as a pencil and the length of three pencils slithered under the picnic table and headed toward the hut. The lady absolutely freaked! "A Snake! A Snake! Kill It! Kill It!"

Ferret face saw his opportunity to be a hero. He started heading toward the snake to stomp it into oblivion! I quickly got between him and the snake. "No! Leave it alone!" The snake slithered under the hut. This didn't please the lady. She had a sleeping bag set up with netting so a snake couldn't possibly get to her. She still wasn't pleased. Ferret face gave me a hostile look with his beady eyes. He should have been taking care of his kids.

After being discharged from the Army in 1973, I hiked the Shenandoahs and passed through Big Meadows Campground. It was fun hiking through the same area in 2009. I could see myself as a young Jim Hill - twenty-five years old - with a lot more red hair and a bright red beard hiking on the same path.

Near Big Meadows Campground I caught up to a group being led by a Forest Ranger. She stopped me and said: "You're a thru-hiker aren't you? I can tell by how small your pack is. Would you mind talking to my group?" "Sure." I just opened it up to questions. Fortunately there were a lot of good ones. They were an enthusiastic group. Who knows, maybe I inspired someone to be a thru-hiker someday.

There were so many places where you could get something to eat right next to the Trail. That ticked me off since I was still carrying a heavy supply of food. The last of these places was the Tom Floyd Wayside. I ordered two cheeseburgers and a blackberry shake. This was right on Skyline Drive and there were tourists inside the store. They smelled of fabric softener and fresh soap. Even I noticed my smell so it must have been pretty bad. The tourists were keeping their distance from me.

After hiking out of the Shenandoah National Park I had no need to stop in Front Royal, Virginia because I still had a five day supply of food. This was a fun day of hiking. I passed farm fields where big rolls of hay were being baled. I passed the National Zoological Park Research Center. It housed exotic animals and was surrounded by a twelve foot fence topped with barbed wire. The forest was thick inside the fence and I didn't see any animals although I did hear some strange animal sounds.

My destination was Dick's Dome shelters. There were two tiny shelters topped with geodesic domes. A stream flowed beside the shelters but the water didn't look good enough to drink untreated. I was low on water and there was a spring next to the Trail about a mile further so I continued on. The woods were super thick in this area and the trail maintainers had done an excellent job of carving a space around the spring. It was a great little spring and the water was crystal clear, cool, and tasted wonderful. I'm sure this was where all the animals came to drink. After filling my water bottles I headed to the campsite twenty yards up the Trail. The Trail maintainers had cut the thick underbrush and left a lovely, grassy, 20 foot by 20 foot space. It was on top of the mountain and there weren't many trees around so I had an unobstructed view of the sky. This was late June and it had been a hot day. It cooled down that evening and the temperature was perfect. I decided to sleep with just the netting covering the tent. Good decision. The stars were beautiful. I was on a flight path to the airports around Washington DC. Every few minutes a plane would come over my tent heading for a landing. I loved it. Tucked into my sleeping blanket and looking up I could see the moving lights of the descending plane against the backdrop of all the twinkling stars.

I remember thinking that after I finished my hike I would be on one of those planes back to Albuquerque, New Mexico. When the stewardess asked for my drink order, I would ask for a coffee with cream and sugar. That sounded so good at the time. (It was as good as I had imagined when it actually happened. It brought back all the memories.)

In the middle of the night, I was awakened by something pushing its way through the dense underbrush. When it made it through it was three feet from my tent. It was startled and perturbed by my presence and let out a couple of sharp exhales. I fumbled for my flashlight. When I finally turned it on the beam reflected off of the netting. By the time I could focus outside the tent the animal was gone. The next morning not twenty feet from my tent a bear left me a greeting. Flies were buzzing around it. It definitely hadn't been there when I went to bed.

When I started hiking the next morning I walked past the black and white fur of a skunk. I learned later after talking to a ridge runner that a thru-hiker had been bitten by the skunk. He had killed the skunk and sought medical treatment. The poor guy had to go through the series of rabies shots. I gave the ridge runner the location of the skunk skin and he was going to pick it up and have it examined.

This was a day I was eagerly looking forward to. Reading hiker's journals over the years, there was a thirteen mile stretch called the "Roller Coaster" that everyone talked about. The Virginia corridor was narrow in this area and the only route was a series of steep climbs and descents over rocky trail. This was when I would find out if the Roller Coaster was actually as tough as the journal writers had described or if they were whiners.

Union Break caught up to me as I was entering the Roller Coaster. I met him on the last day in the Shenandoahs. We both hiked about the same speed and hiked off and on together all the way into southern Pennsylvania. He was twenty-three, had recently graduated from college, and was hiking the Appalachian Trail before starting a career. I enjoyed hiking with him.

This was a hot muggy day. Fortunately there were small streams along the way. I couldn't drink enough water. I emptied my 32 ounce water bottle five times - 160 ounces - during the day's hike. Our destination was the Bears Den Hostel ten miles into the Roller Coaster. I was feeling good and just went full out. Union Break stayed right on my heels. This was rough hiking. It didn't let up. Steep climbs left me drenched with sweat. Equally steep descents gave me a chance to catch my breath, then right back up again. I was in good condition. My recovery time after a climb was good. After five of these climbs and descents, I was still breathing hard on the down hills.

At the first shelter we reached, Union Break met a friend he had hiked with earlier and started hiking with him. I didn't slow down. By the time I reached the Bears Den Hostel at 4:00 pm I was drained. The Roller Coaster had lived up to its reputation. Fortunately the Bears Den Hostel was air conditioned. I put my over-heated body in front of the air conditioner and basked in the cool air.

This was by far my favorite hostel. At the turn of the century it was probably a vacation home for a wealthy family. It was now owned by the Forest Service. It was a beautiful building made of stone. The builders spared no expense on the interior. There were oak floors, a huge fireplace, and a grand dining area.

The hostel hosts were Red Wing, his wife Hopeful, and their three year old daughter Hikelet. Most hostel owners had seen way too many hikers over the years and the last thing they wanted to do was talk hiking. You could see their eyes glaze over if you started to talk about your hike. Red Wing had hiked the AT twice and Hopeful had also hiked the AT. They wanted to talk hiking. Good hosts can make you feel right at home. Redwing and Hopeful did just that. I was the first hiker to arrive. I had no competition for the shower and took a long one. I had not planned on staying at the Bears Den Hostel but so many hikers had talked about it that I stayed. For $25 I got a bunk, shower, laundry, internet, long distance phone calls, a medium pizza, soda, and a pint of Ben and Jerry's Ice Cream. This far into the hike my body didn't care about quality, it wanted Quantity! My calorie intake that evening was over 4,000 calories. I practically inhaled the pizza. A section hiker with not much appetite could only finish half of his pizza. I finished the rest. After a long, hot day, the cold ice cream and cold Coke hit the spot. Every hostel had a hiker box. In these boxes you could find things other hikers no longer wanted. This hiker box had ten big homemade chocolate chip cookies and fourteen Oreos. I demolished those. It had three packages of Ramen Noodles and three Lipton Noodle dishes that I added to my pack. I had a comfortable bunk and slept soundly.

The next morning, refreshed, I continued on my journey. The three remaining miles of the Roller Coaster were not a good way to start the morning but soon they were behind me. As hikers leave Virginia, some try the "four state challenge". They start in Virginia and hike through West Virginia, Maryland, and end in Pennsylvania in one day - a total of forty-one miles. They do a lot of night hiking and are shot for the next couple of days, but a lot of them complete it.

7 HARPERS FERRY, WEST VIRGINIA

My goal for this day was Harpers Ferry, West Virginia. It was the psychological halfway point of the Appalachian Trail. The actual halfway point was another eighty miles. This was where the headquarters of the Appalachian Trail Conservancy was located. At the ATC Headquarters I had my picture taken and put in a scrapbook with my name, address, e-mail address, trail name and start date. By the time thru-hikers reached Harpers Ferry they were down to less than half of their original number.

Leaving Harpers Ferry, it was a seven mile hike to the next shelter. I crossed the Potomac River and entered Maryland. I found a shady spot next to the river to take a break and have some trail mix. Tourists were floating by on inner tubes and it looked fun.

For the next three miles I followed the C&O Canal towpath. One hundred and fifty years ago mules towed barges along this pathway. The towpath was between what was left of the canal and the Potomac River. It was now a bike path and hiking path. It didn't live up to its potential. Most of the canal was filled with trees, weeds, and underbrush, with pockets of stagnant water. Litter cluttered both sides of the pathway. It went under a couple of bridges where cars were stopped for rush hour traffic. I was hiking through the area in the evening and hiking fast to get through it. There were spots along the river that would have been excellent for camping. The vibrations in this area weren't right. I kept going.

I made it to the Ed Garvey shelter just as it was getting dark. I was out of water. The water source was a spring a half mile down a steep trail. I wasn't looking forward to this. It had been a 27 mile day and I could feel it. With my headlamp on I headed down the pathway. The refreshing, clear water was from a piped spring. I filled my water bottles and headed back up. Steeply up. A Boy Scout Troop had most of the camping spaces but I found a good spot in the dark and put up my tent. It was after 9:00 pm. The scouts were winding down and I slept soundly. I caught up again to Birdie and Bubbles after my five day vacation at my sisters. They were friendly. They warned everyone that I would probably get up at 5:30 in the morning. When I left at 8:30 the next morning, they were surprised.

In Maryland and Pennsylvania there were times when the Trail kept us close to civilization. It bothered other hikers but I liked it. It added variety to the hike. I hiked along the backyard fences of homes. One home had a big confederate flag and a big, nasty dog that wanted a piece of me. Even up in the mountains, I could hear lawn mowers, motorcycles, and honking horns.

This was a short eleven mile day. I headed to Boonsboro, Maryland to re- supply. I was back to the Trail by 5:00 pm. I had two options: Option #1 - I could continue on with a heavy pack for another six miles, barely getting to the next shelter before dark. Option #2 - I could hike about 1/8th of a mile to the Dahlgren Backpack Campground that had hot showers and relax the rest of the day. It was a no-brainer.

This was an excellent campground. It was 200 feet long and 30 feet wide, with a smooth level grassy area. There were picnic tables every ten feet with fire rings. I put up my tent, had a shower, cooked a good dinner, and chatted with other thru-hikers. At 8:00 pm I got into my sleeping blanket and started reading my thru-hiker's guidebook to see what was on tap for the next day.

A big, loud, enthusiastic Boy Scout Troop entered our peaceful campsite at 8:15 pm. That meant they had to set up their tents, make their dinners, and prepare for bed before there was going to be any silence. I could hear the curses of other thru-hikers as they approached. Most of them started putting up their tents close to the bathroom and shower area which was about as far as you could get from my tent. Great! Then two scouts decided to tent ten feet from me. I went over to them: "I need to warn you that I am a loud snorer. You might not get much sleep."

Nice cheerful smiles: "That's OK."

"Aaaaarrrrgggg!"

It didn't matter. Pretty soon half the scout troop was tented in my area. I liked sharing camping areas with boy and girl scout troops, youth groups, troubled youth groups, church groups. Without exception they were high energy, enthusiastic, often times dramatic. Modulation wasn't in their vocabulary. They would stand right next to one another and talk at full volume. It was like fourteen Billy's from the OxiClean infomercial all talking at once. That energy often recharged my batteries and centered me. These kids were having a good time. Isn't that the reason I was out here?

I met three people at Dahlgren Backpack Campground who were hiking together - Nature, Dragon Breath, and Android. I hiked with them for three days.

Nature was a very nice lady. I met her in the first part of Maryland, hiked about one half of Pennsylvania with her, and then met her again just before the Whites in New Hampshire. She must have been just behind me from Pennsylvania to New Hampshire. She hiked at a good pace so we hiked off and on together for the next three days. She and Jim Dandy were the two most determined people I met on my hike. The day before, she had fallen and hit her head on a rock. There was a big bump on her forehead. Her wrist was swollen where she had broken her fall. It looked broken to me, but it was just sprained. During the three days I was hiking with her she pulled off a toenail and another one was about ready to come off. She cut her knee earlier in her hike and it had become infected. She was off the Trail for a week and still had to take medications for it. She had other things go wrong with her during the hike. She was deathly afraid of snakes and never overcame that fear. She had to have seen a lot of them. I saw at least thirty. She never quit. She had worked and raised five kids. When the last one left home she started her hike. A thru-hike of the Appalachian Trail was something she had planned for many years. She was truly, "livin' the dream" and it was meeting her expectations. I admired her focus and indomitable spirit.

Dragon Breath was in his mid-twenties. He loved making fires. Every night and sometimes in the morning, he would get a good one going. We needed them like a hole in the head in July, but I enjoyed them. Dragon Breath hurt his back later in Pennsylvania and had to get off of the Trail to recover. He did get back on and summited Katahdin on the 27th of September. After summiting, he probably had to go back to areas he had skipped and hike them. People did that quite a lot. They would summit early to make sure they were able to finish before the cold weather arrived and then go back and hike the areas they had missed.

Android was a big man in his early twenties. He was a computer programmer. He had already lost fifty pounds and was rightfully proud of his weight loss. He was the slowest of the group but was now capable of twenty miles a day. At the end of a day's hike he was by far the most tired but he liked being part of this group and was hanging in there. He made it to New Jersey and came to the conclusion that he wasn't enjoying his hike any more. Nature tried to talk him out of it but he left the Trail.

After leaving Dahlgren Backpack Campground the day began with an immediate climb. We started at 980' and climbed to the Washington Monument at 1,550'. That's right - the Washington Monument. This was the first monument to George Washington built in 1827. It wasn't terribly impressive. It was kind of shaped like an upside down Styrofoam cup and about a third the size of the Washington Monument in Washington DC. I climbed the stairs to the top. There were good views of the countryside. There was a plaque telling of people from a nearby town witnessing a civil war battle from the top of the monument. They must have seen the formations and battle strategies developing in the valley far below and were watching the actual bloodshed of war.

I finished the day at Raven Rock shelter. As I hiked down to the shelter I was in an area where the sun didn't shine in the afternoon. It became darker and darker as I got closer to the shelter. The shelter was dirty and dreary. I noticed a parking lot twenty yards away. Women thru-hikers were warned to stay away from this shelter. Guys from the nearby town came here to party and had harassed women hikers. I found a spring nearby and filled up my water bottles. I didn't want to stay here. There was a spot just off of the Trail I remembered as looking good. I headed back.

I passed a hiker who was tented in this depressing area. He had a little dog letting me know whose territory I was in. I didn't get his name but Nature told me about him. He started hiking on the first day of January. He and his dog hiked the Florida Trail and then started the Appalachian Trail. He had a long, full beard. He looked melancholy. I saw him a couple of times the next day and his demeanor never changed. He had the smallest dog on the Trail. It was a cute little mongrel about the size of my beagle, Fred. I saw the two of them interacting and it made me miss Fred. This was the only dog that didn't carry a pack. The man carried all of his food and water. He was a happy, lively, little dog and the center of the man's life.

When I reached the spot where I was going to put up my tent Nature, Dragon Breath, and Android were already setting up their tents. I joined them. We spent an enjoyable evening making our dinner and chatting beside the campfire.

The next day started with a climb up to High Rock. People were picking wild blueberries. One lady's hands were stained blue and she had a little bag almost completely full of blueberries. It took me a while to start to pick blueberries but once I did I couldn't stop. They were wonderful right off the bush - warm, juicy, flavorful. My eyes were constantly roving for blueberry bushes.

I crossed the Mason/Dixon line and entered Pennsylvania. This day was just good hiking with a lot of climbs and descents and excellent views. I was hiking at an average pace and was passed by Dragon Breath. When I reached the Rocky Mountain shelter at the end of the day, Nature and Dragon Breath were already there. It was obvious what had happened. Dragon Breath told Nature that he was a faster hiker than me. His attitude toward me was not quite disrespectful, but almost. I let it ride. I passed him the next morning while he was taking a break. I knew he was going to try to pass me to prove he was the faster hiker. I hit the accelerator. I stopped at a shelter three hours later, got out my stove, and made some noodles. I was finishing the noodles when Dragon Breath arrived. He didn't say anything but there was a little smile on his face and the "attitude" was gone. Lots of mind games on the Trail.

The hike from Rocky Mountain shelter to Tom's Run shelter was a good, honest, hardworking 19 miles. I was the first to arrive. There was a camping area about twenty yards in front of the shelter. This was one of the most beautiful spots that I camped on my hike. A stream meandered through the campground. I put my tent under a huge pine tree. Tom's Run shelter was built in 1936. People had been enjoying this setting for a long time. There was a log that crossed the stream. I went over to the log, took off my shoes and socks, and dunked my feet in the ice cold mountain water. It was almost painful. I would take my feet out of the water, massage them, and put them back in. When I finished, my feet had such good blood flow they were almost red. They felt great! That night I was close enough to the stream that the sounds of the flowing water lulled me into a rapid, deep, refreshing sleep.

The next day I reached the half-way point. It felt good knowing I had made it halfway. That's about as excited as I got. I still had 1,089 miles to go.

Near the half-way point there is a tradition called the half-gallon challenge. If you are able to accomplish it, you get a tiny wooden spoon and become an official member of the "half gallon club". The challenge takes place at the Pine Grove General Store in Pine Grove Furnace State Park. The participants choose their flavor and then start trying to eat a half gallon of ice cream. When I arrived, the only person taking the challenge was Spider. He was half-way through and noticeably slowing down. I wimped out and didn't take the challenge. Instead, I ordered a cheeseburger and chocolate malt and enjoyed the show. Spider was now ¾ of the way through. He was perspiring and starting to look a little nauseous. Nature, Android, and Dragon Breath showed up together. Nature and Android passed, but Dragon Breath took the challenge. The guy was good. He downed his ice cream at an even pace. He almost finished before Spider. Spider finished and quickly headed to the bathroom.

Everyone was talking about Blackbird. He had finished the half gallon challenge and left just before I got there. Fletch was the first "character" I met on the Trail. Blackbird was the second. To me, for a person to be a character, they have to be genuine. They can't be trying to be a character. I introduced Blackbird earlier with his sixty pound pack and $110 grocery bill. Somehow I didn't notice it, but he wore a beanie. Whenever his name was mentioned, people would always say: "Oh Yea. That's the guy with the beanie." He was a little guy, not much bigger than me. His sixty pound pack looked huge on him. I know I couldn't have carried it. Everyone at one time or another tried to talk him out of that heavy pack. I even tried. He said he wanted to start hiking twenty mile days. I suggested that he eat down his food supply and then keep no more than five days of food in his pack. Lighter weight = more speed. He very politely said - no. He was in his mid-twenties, from a small town in Iowa, and seemed to have some of those Midwestern values - hardworking, stubborn, frugal. At the mention of Blackbird everyone had a story of how much they had seen him eat. Most thru-hikers had lost considerable weight by the time they reached New Hampshire. They were rail thin, had gaunt faces, and bony shoulders. When Blackbird reached New Hampshire he had gained seven pounds. To me that was incredible. He hiked ten hours a day, day after day, month after month. He hiked up and down mountains with a sixty pound pack. The calorie bum had to have been enormous. So now was the moment of truth. How would Blackbird handle the half gallon challenge?

He ate two half gallons of ice cream and washed it down with a bag of chips and two hot dogs.

That was a fun 19 mile day that ended at Alec Kennedy shelter. Six relatives were visiting Miles at this shelter. It was their first and last day on the Trail. They were sore but in good spirits. Like most day hikers they brought way too much excellent food. Somebody had to eat the leftovers.........Burp!

The next day I hiked 26 miles. It started with a climb to Center Point Knob and an excellent view of Pennsylvania farm land. I headed down a beautiful trail to Boiling Springs, Pennsylvania. The Trail passed a pond where people were walking their dogs. One kid had a remote control motor boat and was terrorizing the ducks. I stopped at the Mid Atlantic Office of the ATC. It was right on the Trail and was closed since it was Saturday. There was a hiker box next to the entrance. I found a couple of power bars but mainly there were canned goods - beans, peaches, pears, chili. Most hikers stayed away from the weight of canned goods. A hiker was there stuffing himself with the canned goods. He would jam his knife into a can and rip around the edges to open it. I was waiting for him to cut himself. He was eating as fast as he could and furtively glancing to his right and left. I couldn't understand his emotions. We were the only ones there. I had no interest in the canned goods. The cans were for hikers. He could have eaten them all and nobody would have cared. He was still eating when I left.

The Trail headed out of town and crossed over the Pennsylvania Turnpike. I started walking through miles and miles of cornfields. Fortunately the corn wasn't yet as high as an elephant's eye, but the thought inspired me, and glancing around to make sure I didn't have an audience, I sang in my best Robert Goulet baritone: "Oh What A Beautiful Morning. Oh What A Beautiful Day. I've Got A beautiful Feeling Everything's Going My Way. The Cattle Are Standing Like Statues. The Cattle Are Standing Like Statues. The Corn Is As High As An Elephants Eye And The Little

Gray Mare Is Winking Her Eye. Oh What A Beautiful Morning. Oh What A Beautiful Day. I've Got A Beautiful Feeling Everything's Going My Way. Oh What A Beautiful Day!" And it was a beautiful day.

For about a mile the Trail went back into the woods. I walked by a 30 foot x 30 foot family cemetery. It was surrounded by a well-crafted three foot stone wall. The earliest graves dated back to the 1820's. They became more and more fancy with time. Maybe the Campbell family was becoming prosperous. The last headstone was dated 1898 and made of granite. There was still room for more graves. I wonder what happened?

I arrived at the Cove Mountain shelter after a 25.5 mile day. Blue Rey was already there. We had leapfrogged most of the day. We were the only two at the shelter and it was like talking to a mirror image. He talked about loving to hike in fog and described the mist as soothing and energizing. Over and over he would say things that were exactly my thoughts. I enjoyed his company.

The next day's destination was Duncannon, Pennsylvania. The Trail headed right through town. I stopped at Mutzabaugh's Market to re-supply. It had a deli and I was very hungry so I ordered a roast beef sandwich and coke before I started grocery shopping. I sat down at a table to eat my sandwich. I was feeling a little self-conscious because I knew I had the hiker stench. Eight retired men were having their daily coffee at a couple of tables next to mine. One of them said: "You've got to be a thru-hiker, you've got the look." When I said yes, they all started asking questions. They put me at ease. I could tell they were glad to have one of their own hiking the Trail. They really pepped me up.

The Doyle Hotel in Duncannon, Pennsylvania was a "destination." Hikers of all ages stopped for at least a beer. The ones who wanted to party knew this was the place. Those that partied hard had stories to tell around the campfire for the rest of the hike – and did.

8 THE ROCKS OF PENNSYLVANIA

"The Rocks of Pennsylvania" started in earnest after Duncannon. Having read many Trail Journal entries of hikers dealing with the rocks, I knew it was going to be challenging. They talked of small, sharp rocks that shredded your boots and trail runners. (By the end of Pennsylvania I was tearing pieces off of the bottom of both of my hiking shoes. I had purchased them in Waynesboro, Virginia less than three weeks earlier.) On many occasions, I would slide my foot between small rocks at an angle and put my weight on it. Talk about major pain! That had me cussing a lot!

There were small, sharp, rocks combined with wobbly, bigger, rocks where I had to jump from rock to rock. If I slipped and fell, I fell on sharp rocks. (I had cuts on the shin of my left leg, on both knees, and both arms.)

Sometimes the rocky Trail went steeply up for half a mile. I would be climbing from rock to rock or boulder to boulder, looking for a place to get a hand hold or foothold. There were entire days when the Trail was nothing but rocks. These days were mentally and physically tiring. The concentration had to be total. I would be looking down all day and using my hiking poles 100% of the time. Many times I had to jam my poles down hard to break a fall. At the end of the day my arms and hands ached from holding the poles so tightly. Imagine driving on a freeway in a snowstorm for nine hours and you get the idea of the mental fatigue.

I watched timid hikers hesitate before making a jump from rock to rock where a slip and fall would hurt them. For a few thru-hikers, I wondered if it was within their ability to not hurt themselves on the rocks. I was ahead of them so I never found out.

The rocks had an infinite number of ways to torment me. Mercifully my mind has started to eliminate them from my memory. Many people ended their hike in Pennsylvania, either from injury or just the mental and physical fatigue of dealing with so many ROCKS!

The rocks of Pennsylvania were the turning point of my hike. Once I hit the rocks, my ability to hike fast was gone. Hiking fast over rocks was jarring on my body. I had to use my hiking poles way too many times to keep from falling. Whenever I hiked over rocks I slowed way down. I had to stay within my ability and I had very little ability. Some people seemed to glide over the rocks as they passed me. I wanted to shoot them a raspberry!

Before the rocks, my thru-hike had been challenging but there was nothing that slowed me down. I had not missed a day because of illness or injury. Twenty plus mile days were the rule, not the exception. This was a very frustrating time. My goal was to complete my thru- hike in four months - April 28th to August 28th. I needed to average 18 miles a day to do this. From the time I left my sisters on June 19th until I reached Duncannon, Pennsylvania on July 4th, I averaged 18.6 miles per day. For the next 18 days from Duncannon to Kent, Connecticut, I wrote down the number of miles I hiked each day. If there was a re-supply day and I only made 12 miles, I would hike extra hours the next day to bring my average back to 18. Averaging 18 miles a day became an obsession. The long days were physically and mentally draining. There were times I would shuffle slowly along with no energy at all.

It took way too long to re-define my goal. Kent, Connecticut was where I finally slowed my hike down. When I did, it was like a breath of fresh air. I was still thoroughly enjoying my hike but once I slowed it down, I enjoyed it that much more. By going fast from the start, I had given myself a good cushion. I didn't have to worry at all about arriving at Mount Katahdin before the snow. From then on my goal was to listen to my body. If I wanted to hike a long day, I did. If I wanted to hike a short day, I did. Mainly I hiked form 8:00 am or 9:00 am to 6:00 pm or 7:00 pm, and it felt great not having a "deadline" hanging over me.

When I left Duncannon, the Trail went right through the residential part of town. This was a blue collar town. I passed a lot of well cared for homes. It was the 4th of July. People were mowing their lawns and getting their homes ready for barbeques and festivities. I crossed the Susquehanna River on a long bridge. A gust of wind had me quickly grabbing my hat. I entered the forest and started an eight mile climb to Table Rock. I stopped at Peter's Mountain shelter. There were 300 rock steps down to a spring. My legs could feel it coming back up. I was thirsty and drank a lot of water while making dinner. I had to go back for more water the next morning and wasn't too pleased.

The day started with a climb on a rocky pathway. The views at the top were worth the effort. For the next couple of miles I hiked on rock slabs and hopped from boulder to boulder. When I passed this rocky area, the

Trail followed an old grass covered mountain road. There was a man lying in the shade of a small tree. He had his leg propped up. He was close to 280 pounds and at least 60 pounds overweight. He was a day hiker. He wasn't sure if he had sprained his ankle or broken it. He had a cell phone and had called 911. A rescue party was on its way. He had been there for over two hours and was out of water. I had 32 ounces in one of my water bottles and filled his empty one. I asked him if he wanted me to stay until the paramedics arrived. He said he would be ok. He didn't look or sound like he was hurting too much. It was probably only a sprain. It didn't look swollen or at an odd angle.

I continued on my hike. I noticed that he was very lucky. This was one of the few areas where the Trail wasn't steep, winding, and rocky. I hiked on for another mile. I saw the rescue group heading toward me in an ATV with a stretcher on the back. There were four of them. I answered their questions and told them they were about a mile from the injured hiker.

I continued my hike. Another ATV headed toward me with four more paramedics. I answered their questions and they headed on their way.

I continued my hike. Here comes another ATV. It's the Chief and his assistant - The Main Man. He was busy talking on the phone to the paramedics ahead and gave me a brief nod as he passed.

I continued on my hike. You've got to be kidding! Here comes another ATV. I don't know who these people were. When I reached the trailhead, there were two fire trucks and two ambulances, all with their lights flashing. Talk about overkill! I remember thinking: "These people have way too much time on their hands!" I hope the poor guy didn't get charged for all of this.

The Trail passed an old mining village. Not much was left, just small stonework of what was once the foundation of homes. I walked around for a while trying to get a feel for what it must have been like when this was a little village. Ten yards from the Trail I came across an old tree. Three feet from the bottom of the tree was a little round knot about an inch in diameter. It became the mouth. A nose, mustache, and little round eyes were added. It was cute. It was so worn with age it was barely visible. It had to have been over a hundred years old. I wonder how much older than that?

I ended the day at Rausch Gap shelter. Blackbird was already there and had his gear set up in the shelter. Soon Crickey joined us. We were the only ones at the shelter that night. We made our dinners and chatted. After dinner, Crickey found a place to put his tent fifty yards from the shelter. It was almost dark. He came back to the shelter and asked if I was going to be tenting. He had heard an animal close by that was perturbed by his presence and had snorted a couple of times. I couldn't help it. I told of the bear encounter outside of Hot Springs, North Carolina and of the situation that sounded similar to his in the Shenandoahs. Crickey and Blackbird listened quietly. I imitated the snorts I had heard in the Shenandoahs. Crickey said: "That's what I heard." I found a spot about twenty feet from Crickey's tent. I could see he was relieved to have me tenting in the same area. Pretty soon Blackbird quietly joined us and set up his tent nearby.

The next morning I navigated through fields of corn and around cattle in pastures. In the afternoon it started to get nasty. There was a big climb from 450' to 1,300' on rock. The Trail stayed rocky the rest of the day. It took total concentration. If there was even a slight lapse of concentration, just taking my eyes off of the pathway to look at a bird, I would pay the price with either a jammed foot or semi-spectacular save with the hiking poles. It was a long, difficult, twenty-three mile day. I put up my tent in the dark and found a beautiful spot between two streams under tall pine trees. There was even a picnic table where I set up my stove and made dinner. I was pleasantly surprised to see Crickey's headlamp light bobbing in the distance.

The next morning I had to brush back some moss to fill my water bottle. The water had an earthy smell. I took a gulp. It had an earthy taste. I dumped it out. That day I didn't feel 100%. I only hiked ten miles. I didn't have to re-supply. I took off at a normal time from Hertlein Campsite. I just fought with the rocks all day long. I would only hike as fast as the rocks would allow and it was a brutal day. Crickey left the Trail at the nearest road and hitched into town. He had a tick bite on his elbow he thought was starting to show the bulls eye mark of Lyme disease and was going to get it checked. There was a lot of grass next to the Trail in Pennsylvania loaded with ticks. I pulled off four ticks in Pennsylvania and I would heavily coat my socks and legs with Deet each morning.

I reached Eagles Nest shelter at 6:00 pm. Freebird was there. I had last seen him fifty miles before Waynesboro, Virginia. Freebird looked like a swashbuckler. Give him a sword and he would have been one of the Three Muscateers. He was big. He had hair that came to his shoulders. He wore a kilt. Call it what you want, it looked like a skirt. I don't think too many people would have argued the point with him. He had leather boots that must have weighed a ton. The right boot was so worn that the heel support was gone and he was walking on the leather of the boot. I don't know how he kept his balance but he made hiking the rocks look easy. Because of the boot, when he walked, his shoulders would roll from side to side, almost like a swagger. Swashbuckler!

From Eagles Nest shelter I hiked eight miles to Port Clinton, Pennsylvania. The Trail went through Port Clinton. I needed to re-supply but they didn't have a grocery. I headed back into the mountains and an 800' climb to Pocahontas Spring. Just before Pocahontas Spring I passed Clyde. He was less than ten feet off of the Trail and his back was to me. He was bending down and his underwear were still on but in two seconds they wouldn't be. I made some noise and he turned around. That's how I met Clyde. I didn't get any better. I continued hiking and he caught up to me just before I reached Pocahontas Spring. This was a beautiful little box spring about a foot deep and two feet square. I took out my water bottles to fill them. Clyde dipped his water bottle into the spring before I had a chance to. He put his whole hand down into the water. Knowing what his hand had been doing less than ten minutes earlier, I passed on getting water.

My destination was Windsor Furnace shelter. I had it all to myself. I enjoyed a hot dinner, put up my tent with just the netting, and placed it inside the shelter. This would make it much quicker to pack in the morning, protect me from mosquitoes, and keep the mice away. It was a pleasant night. The stars were out. I could hear the melancholy hoot of an owl. I drifted into a peaceful sleep.

I was awakened by a light flashing in my face. It was 12:30 in the morning. It was Clyde. He was out of water and asked to borrow some of mine. He took out his stove and made his dinner. After dinner he sat back, relaxed, and had a cigarette. By this time I had had enough. I gathered my gear and headed to a camping spot. It didn't occur to him that he was being inconsiderate. This wasn't my night. I set up my tent under a tree and pissed off a squirrel. It kept dropping pine cones around my tent for the next hour.

I hadn't had a good re-supply since Mutzabaugh's Grocery store before Duncannon, Pennsylvania. I decided to stop in Walnutport, Pennsylvania. It was still morning so the first thing I did was have a big breakfast at McDonalds. They have a 1,200 calorie beauty with two big pancakes, syrup, butter, hash browns, two pieces of toast, two jelly packets, and scrambled eggs. That didn't quite do it, so I had a breakfast burrito and coffee. After re-supplying I was still hungry so on the way back to the Trail I stopped at Burger King. They had coffee and a big cinnamon roll that looked good. When I walked in the door with my pack, I noticed I was the only customer. There were three ladies at the counter. One was my age and the other two were in their fifties. I heard one of them say under her breath. "I saw him first!"

One of the ladies said something in a low voice and the other two chuckled wickedly. I had their undivided attention. "Are you a thru-hiker?" "Yes." "What's your trail name?" "Wingo." "How far have you hiked?" "1,200 miles." "How many miles do you have left?" "About 1,000 miles." "Wow! Aren't you tired?" "A little bit, but I'm hangin' in there." "You must have a lot of muscles." Wink. "Sure do." Smile. Wink. Fortunately my cinnamon roll and coffee arrived. I wasn't sure how much longer Mr. Sex Appeal could keep this up. When I left I waved and said: "Goodbye,

Ladies." Smiles: "Bye, Wingo." They made me feel good.

I headed back to the Trail. It was 11:00 am by the time I was hiking again and it was already a hot day. I hiked about 100 yards and found a big flat slab of rock in the shade of a giant oak tree. The rock was cool to the touch. I took off my pack and lay on my back looking up at the clouds. The muscles in my back automatically relaxed and seemed to sink into the cool rock. Soon I was snoring peacefully. I was awakened by my own snoring. I stayed there for a while, completely relaxed, staring up at the passing clouds. I needed that break because the rest of the day was a doozy!

The area I was hiking in had been devastated by nearly a century of zinc smelting. The whole mountain at one time was treeless and vegetation and water sources had been contaminated. It became a Superfund site in 1982 and was making a comeback. Small trees were starting to grow on the slopes and bushes were covering the ground, including blueberry bushes with plump blueberries. They were tempting but I passed.

Sometimes to get a conversation going around a campfire I would ask what were some of the most memorable parts of the Trail. The climb I was about to start was mentioned often. I agree. This was a hairy climb. There were no trees. It was up the side of a mountain. It was all rocks and boulders. I would look at a rock face and say to myself: "How the hell do I get up this thing? People before me have, so there must be a way." I would stare at the rock and figure out handholds and footholds and finally get over it. This happened over and over. Once, I had to slide around a boulder while trying to keep my pack weight from toppling me over the side. The area wasn't well marked and I ended up making an even more precarious climb to a ridge high above. When I reached the top the views were spectacular. I could see the town where I had re-supplied and three other towns along the river. There was an airport next to one of the towns and the landing strip pointed in my direction. I watched a small plane take off and fly overhead. I could see the pilot. There were mining operations with big smelters that looked like they were still in operation. I watched an Amtrac train go by on the tracks far below. All the mountains in this area had seen way too much mining.

As I was enjoying the view I had a snack and drank more water than I should have. The Appalachian Trail was re-routed in this area and the re-route by-passed the water source I was counting on. I only had 16 ounces of water for the rest of the hot day.

Ned The Fed caught up to me. I had been reading his shelter journal entries since early Virginia. I was within a day of catching him just before I took five days off at my sisters. Ned The Fed hiked portions of the Trail in 2005 and kept a journal on TrailJournal.com. It was a well written journal. He was keeping a journal this year, too. I read it for a couple of weeks before starting my hike. He had a list of things to take on the hike and after reading that list, I added a couple of items to my pack. Ned The Fed wasn't so much a "character" as he was a "force" on the Trail. Hikers listened to him as a man of experience. I think he was a retired FBI agent. We chatted for a while and then parted ways. I leapfrogged with Ned The Fed all the way through New Jersey, New York, Connecticut, Massachusetts, Vermont and the first part of New Hampshire, and never once saw him again. He made it all the way to Maine, his knee gave out, and he had to leave the Trail. So much effort to hike that far. So agonizingly close!

I hiked along a ridgeline for five miles. It was hot and I was really thirsty. I was now down to four ounces of water. There was a shelter with water in four miles and a turn off to a spring in one mile. I opted for the spring even though it was a half mile down a steep trail. It was really steep. The spring was in a shady area and there was a bountiful flow of cold water. I was so thirsty I filled and emptied my water bottle twice - 64 ounces - before I quenched my thirst. I filled my water bottles and drank some more before heading out.

The steep climb back to the Trail was no fun. I slipped on a loose rock and grabbed a small tree. The tree gave way and the trunk barely missed me as it fell down the slope. A branch nicked my arm as it went by and left a long bloody scratch. Neosporin to the rescue.

Once re-hydrated, my energy level picked up again. I passed Fat Kid. Fat Kid was anything but fat and never had been. He had to have been tired of answering the question: "Did you lose a lot of weight?" He started hiking with a friend of his. His friend was hyper-energetic and eventually hiked the Trail in about 90 days. Fat Kid just wanted to hike at a normal speed which frustrated hyper-energetic. Hyper-energetic started calling him Fat Kid - the one you always have to slow down for. The two split early in their hike.

Fat Kid had one of the best attitudes on the Trail. His shelter journal entries were always humorous and positive. He looked and sounded like a twenty year old Jay Leno. He liked to talk to everyone. Everyone liked him. I saw him many times from Pennsylvania to the end of my hike. Each time it was a pleasure seeing him. I might not see him for three weeks but when we re-united he remembered what we had been talking about and it was like we just continued the conversation. He hit about every party on and off the Trail. He took time off to go to weddings. He lived in New York City and had friends visit and hike with him when he reached New York state. He probably stayed at half the hostels on the Trail. He was one of the few people I would hike with for a full day. He reminded me a lot of Rocky. He was having a ball.

My next destination was Delaware Water Gap. Hikers looked forward to DWG because it was supposed to have an excellent bakery. It did. I started with freshly baked, soft, yet crisp chocolate chip cookies. There was an apple pastry that looked delicious. It was. I had an excellent beef burrito and finished it off with a mocha latte. The place was packed with tourists and hikers and it should have been. Good food.

Before heading back to the Trail I stopped at the outfitters. Earlier in the day I had tried to break my fall by planting my hiking pole. It slid out from under my weight and I went down heavily. I knew the tips of my hiking poles were wearing out but after the rocks of Pennsylvania they were down to little nubs. The outfitter replaced the tips for me and I could feel an immediate difference. I spent the next hour spearing leaves with my new sharp tips.

9 NEW JERSEY

After leaving Delaware Water Gap I headed across the Delaware River Bridge into New Jersey. This was a lovely old bridge high above the water. The river was wide and curved after it passed the bridge. It was a breezy day and little boats were bobbing in the water. The whole area was surrounded by thick green forest. It reminded me of the cover of a jigsaw puzzle box.

I had a pre-conceived idea of what hiking in New Jersey was going to be like - not much forest and way too many people. The first two miles played right into my prejudice. There was a beautiful recreation area along the river. This was a Saturday right at the peak of tourist season. You couldn't have stuffed more people into the area. The picnic tables were filled. Those not lucky enough to have a picnic table, put blankets on the ground where they had their food spread out. The activity and noise level was high and it was kind of overwhelming after having spent so much time in the quiet of the forest.

"I told you so!" I said to myself smugly. I entered back into the forest on a wide pathway that paralleled a small stream for a couple of miles. There were a lot of people hiking in this area. They all seemed to be enjoying this gorgeous day. I felt a good energy. I loved seeing so many people enjoying what I enjoy. I enjoyed listening to people talking with their New Jersey and New York accents. The delivery had an attitude - tough talking.

I need to clear something up right away: New Jersey amazed me. Time after time I would reach a mountain top with a 360 degree view and the only thing I could see in any direction was forest.

The mountains were loaded with blueberry bushes. I had become a blueberry fan and I loved it. Blueberries were a good source of food for bears. There were more bears in New Jersey than any other state. All the shelters had warnings of aggressive bears. It seems like all the thru-hikers except me, knew ways of staying away from the shelters in New Jersey. The ex-mayor of Unionville, New Jersey opened his home to thru-hikers. They even had dinner and breakfast with the mayor. I heard nothing but good things about this generous man. In a couple of towns, hikers could tent at the town pavilion or next to the fire station.

I spent my first night in New Jersey at the Backpacker Campsite. This was a spacious campsite in a grassy meadow with pine trees here and there for shade. I found a good spot and set up my tent. This campground had a bear box so I didn't have to hang my food bag.

A group of troubled teens had their tents set up about thirty feet away. I listened to them interacting positively with their counselors. One of the teens had a slight stutter and I could tell he didn't want to be the center of attention. As he was talking to the group, everyone was quiet and respectful. He got through it and I could almost feel his increase in confidence.

There were three tents set up twenty feet to the south of me. I nodded to the campers but didn't say anything to them. From their accents, they were from New York or New Jersey. They looked like novice hikers. They combined their food bags into one huge food bag and hung it on a tree branch right next to their tents. The bag was only about seven feet off of the ground.

I liked my comfortable, grassy location, there were a lot of people at the campsite, even a ridge runner in charge of the campground, so I let my defenses down and went into a peaceful sleep. I dreamed there was a bear walking by my tent. It had a terrible odor. Its stomach was growling, and it brushed against my tent.

I heard a heavy thud and something rushed by my tent. I became fully awake. I could hear a constant grinding sound in the distance and couldn't figure out what it was. I unzipped my tent and looked out. The three men were outside their tents looking confused. The bear had knocked their food bag down from the tree and stolen it. It stayed in the campground for a couple of hours eating the food. I think the grinding sound was its teeth grinding on cans to open them.

In my sleep, my mind had been recording the rancid smelling bear brush my tent with its nose as it sniffed for food, and the sound of its growling stomach. My mind never went on High Alert. It just continued to record. It wasn't until the bear rushed by my tent with the food that I became fully awake. I know if I had been camping alone I would have been instantly on High Alert!

The next day the Trail continued to be wide and relatively smooth to Sunfish Pond. I sat on a bench beside the glacial pond and enjoyed the stillness of the early morning. There was an occasional - brrraaappp - from a bullfrog. The sun was beginning to rise, creating beautiful reflections of the surrounding trees on the water. There was a plaque that made me smile. It declared this lovely glacial pond to be the seventh wonder of.............................New Jersey! There was a climb to Catfish Fire Tower. From the tower I experienced the first of many panoramic views of New Jersey. I walked along a ridge for the next three miles and stopped to talk to Two-Pound and her hiking partner as they were taking a break. They were heading to a screened-in shelter next to Long Pond and invited me to join them. It was .8 miles off Trail so I passed. I should have joined them.

My destination was Brink Road shelter. It was deep in the woods and the trees were close together. When I reached the shelter it was a lot darker than it should have been at 7:00 pm. The shelter was dirty. I looked at the shelter journal and bears were mentioned too often in the previous week. The AT Thru-Hikers' Companion guidebook said: "Bears are especially active here." I was all by myself…. I think you are noticing a build-up to a "Cluck, cluck, cluck!" Yes indeed! I chickened out!

It was only four miles to Branchville, New Jersey. From there I could walk on U.S. 206 to a motel two miles away and spend the night. By the time I reached U.S. 206 I had been using my headlamp for an hour. I went east on U.S. 206 and headed to the motel. I had my headlamp on so that cars could see me. There was no sidewalk and it was a tight shoulder. The temperature was getting cooler so I put on my yellow rain jacket. When I reached the motel it was full and the lights were out. It was 10:00 pm and noticeably cooler. I added my fleece pullover. The next motel was four miles in the opposite direction. I had been hiking since 7:00 am and was starting to feel it. I turned around and headed west. I was at an intersection looking kind of miserable when a truck stopped. The man rolled down his window and said: "Can I help you?" I told him my dilemma. He was actually planning to go in another direction, but he said: "Get in." He was a firefighter just getting off of work. He drove me to the Forest Motel. He told me to go in and make sure they had a room. If they didn't, he said he would figure something out. Fortunately there was a room. I couldn't thank him enough. Kindnesses like this happened over and over on the Trail.

The Forest Motel was in its prime in the 40's. What the heck. I was tired. The price was right. It had a shower and a bed with clean sheets - And No Bears! I took a soothing hot shower; then slept until 9:00 am. Check-out time was 11:00 am and I lounged around watching TV until it was time to go.

It's hard to imagine what a treat staying at a motel was for me. I stayed at five motels the whole trip. Being completely clean for a change, smelling good, not being bothered by bugs, mosquitoes, or mice, not having to be alert to the sounds of the night, having a room all to myself - staying at motels greatly improved my morale.

The next morning I walked 1.8 miles uphill back to the trailhead. I turned down a ride from one of the guests at the motel because I thought a nearby restaurant was open. It wasn't and I cussed for the next hour as I trudged up the hill. I headed to Jumboland Restaurant. I had two excellent breakfasts and stuffed myself so much I was actually full.

It was a good thing because I hiked almost continuously from Branchville, New Jersey to Vernon, New Jersey - 34.9 Trail miles. If the mileage from the Forest Motel to Jumboland Restaurant and back to the trailhead, and the mileage from the trailhead to Vernon, New Jersey - 6.2 miles - is included, I traveled 41.1 miles. And you thought impetuousness was just for young hikers. Move over you two young hikers with your 41 mile day into Damascus, Virginia. Move over all you people who completed the 41 mile "four state challenge" in one day. Make room for Wingo! He is just as crazy as you are!

I hadn't planned on hiking that far. I started my hike at 2:00 pm and was planning to stop at the Rutherford shelter twelve miles up the Trail. When I was within a mile of the shelter it was after 8:00 pm and it was a beautiful evening. The sun was beginning to set and the clouds were a soft red. I remember thinking: "I want to keep going." It was that impulsive.

I hiked until almost 9:00 pm without using my headlamp. I could just see the outline of the pathway. I stumbled and barely caught my balance with my hiking poles and decided to turn on the headlamp. It was a good little headlamp. The beam was bright and it had a good range. It had four settings. I put it on the brightest setting.

It was definitely different, hiking at night. The sounds were magnified. I remember hearing crickets first; then they became a constant background noise. It became cool and I started to see my breath in the beam of the headlamp. I dug into my pack and found my fleece pullover. I added my yellow rain jacket. With both on I thought I might be too warm but it was just right. Bugs were attracted to the beam of light from my headlamp. There were a lot of them. They would bump into me. I brushed them off of my clothes and from in back of my neck. All the bugs attracted a bat. It stayed with me for at least an hour, darting in and out of the beam of my headlamp. I would see a shadow quickly dart through the light and hear a "snap" - got another one!

A calmness came over me in the darkness. I breathed deeply and relaxed. I was truly living in the moment. I slowed down to make sure I didn't fall. I would shine the light a little bit ahead of where I stepped, not right down at my feet. It doesn't sound like it would work, but it did. I concentrated on staying on the Trail.

The Appalachian Trail is marked with white blazes. They are about three inches wide and six inches long and are painted on trees at about eye level.

If the Trail converges or if there is something ahead that requires your attention, the tree will have two white blazes.

Some states do a beautiful job of marking their Trail with the white blazes, others don't. New Jersey did a pretty good job. Sometimes the blazes would be every 50 to 100 feet and other times you could walk a quarter mile without seeing one. That's when anxiety would creep in: "Did I make a wrong turn? C'mon! Show up! Whew! There it is!" When the light from my headlamp hit the blazes, they became bright little beacons in the night.

The Trail would fade out at times. There might be a wide area or rocky area where I couldn't see the pathway. I would continue on the same course and wait for the dirt footpath to show up again. Sometimes a white blaze would show up in the distance and I would head toward it knowing I would intercept the Trail.

I had no depth perception. When my breathing became rapid, I was in a climb. There were tricky, steep descents over rocks. I had an easier time descending at night than during the day. The beam of light focused exactly where I needed to put my foot and didn't show how far the drop was if I fell.

After a couple of hours I turned off my headlamp and took a break. I was high in the Appalachian Mountains. Alone. There was no sound. Totally still. No cricket noise. Nothing. I looked up. I could see the outline of tall trees. The only illumination was coming from a sky full of bright stars. Full! I have never seen so many stars! It was absolutely Gorgeous! I stood motionless for a long time staring at the stars. What were my feelings at this time? Very basic. I was glad to be alive. There are moments I know will last forever. This was one of them.

A half hour later I came around a curve and saw a big object on a mountaintop in the distance. It looked like the Washington Monument. There were spotlights shining on it. It was unexpected and startling. I learned later it was called High Point Monument and honored those who died in war. I had never heard of it but it was impressive. There were a couple of decent sized cities nearby whose lights created a soft glow in the darkness.

I passed an observation platform that I didn't go up. It was closing in on 1:00 in the morning and I knew if I did, I would curl up on the wooden floor and go to sleep. I was enjoying this night hike. Sometimes the sounds of the night intruded. I would hear the loud snap of a branch and my flight or fight instincts would kick in. Once I heard something moving in the distance. I stood completely still to hear if it was heading toward me. I couldn't tell, so I walked faster to get out of its territory. I remember hearing the hoot of an owl. I love that sound. We were sharing the night.

I heard movement in the bushes to my left and turned my head toward the sound. Two absolutely gorgeous yellow eyes sparkled like emeralds in the lamplight. The eyes were about waist high. They didn't blink and stayed perfectly still.

I stopped at the High Point State Park Headquarters to get a drink of water. It was 2:00 am and everything was closed. There was a little camera that was motion sensitive. I felt kind of paranoid, sitting on the park bench eating my trail mix with the camera staring at me.

I had a hard time finding the trailhead after my break. It wasn't well marked. After a ten minute search I found it. I was starting to stumble occasionally. The Trail seemed more difficult. It felt like there were a lot more climbs and descents. There were too many stream crossings. I was starting to feel tired.

I lost the Trail. I walked ahead looking to the left and right searching for a white blaze. No luck. The Trail headed in a north/south direction. I began what I hoped was an east/west pattern to intercept the Trail. This was a fairly flat area with an old rock boundary wall. No luck. I widened the east/west pattern. I knew my tenacity would sooner or later be rewarded. I searched for over an hour. I had scratches all over my legs from the fallen branches I had brushed against. I ran into a fire trail and followed it for a couple of hundred yards until I came to a field. I remembered walking through a field so I followed a grassy tractor pathway in the direction I thought the Trail would be. By the time I reached the end of the field there was no sign of the Trail.

I was tired and frustrated and decided to take a break on the grassy pathway, even get a little shuteye if I could. I was uncomfortably close to a farmer's house. I couldn't see the house but I could hear a dog barking. It was a deep bark. The field was fallow. It had thick long grass. The tractor pathway was matted down enough so I could lie down. I stretched out and closed my eyes. I immediately felt things crawling on my legs. I flashed the light on my legs and there were ticks crawling all over them. I quickly brushed them off and pulled off a couple of stubborn ones. I very quietly took my tent out of my pack and put it together with just the netting. I kept expecting the dog to start barking more and hear the farmer yell: "What's Going On Over There?"

I checked myself and all my gear for ticks and climbed into the tent. I was tired but I was too wound up to sleep. I stayed in my tent for an hour and a half. By 5:30 am there was enough light to see again and I headed back to find the Trail. It took a while but I found it. What a relief.

It's odd, but as it became daylight, my body began to wake up. I had my Pop Tarts and trail mix for breakfast and continued hiking. I'm almost glad I got lost. The next two hours were through a beautiful swamp where I walked over wooden bog bridges that were rickety at times. I hiked through fields and by a farmhouse next to the Trail that had a big, aggressive dog.

I'm glad I didn't have to mess with that in the night.

I continued on to Unionville, New Jersey where I stopped and had a much needed coffee. The rest of the hike from Unionville, New Jersey to Vernon, New Jersey took about six hours. I don't remember much about it. I put my head down and started grinding out the miles. I was weary, fatigued, and it seemed like it took forever to hike twelve miles.

I passed an impressive footbridge before reaching N.J. 94. It was over a swamp that had more color than I expected and a variety of birds. N.J. 94 headed east for three miles to Vernon, however, fifty yards to the west was Heaven Hill Farm. It had all kinds of goodies. I had the home-made ice cream. Delicious. I had seconds. I had a pear, apple, and a big cup of coffee.

Vernon had a hostel run by St. Thomas Episcopal Church. I hadn't been to a church hostel before. I had a good stay. A $10 donation was requested but I had to search for the donation box. The hostel was in the basement of the church. It was spacious and clean. It was blocked off into two areas. A smaller area had a computer and television with DVD and VCR. There was a table with chairs around it. On top of the table parishioners had kindly left food that they baked for the hikers. A sliding partition separated the smaller area from the larger area which had a kitchen. There was a clean bathroom and shower area. The rules were clearly written out. We had to read them and sign them - no drinking, smoking, foul language, and lights out by 10:00 pm.

I met hikers I would see for the rest of my hike: Hobbit and Knickers were sisters in their mid- twenties. They were hiking with Hobbit's dog Jumar who was the best trained dog I have seen in my life. Bill Senior and Bill Junior were father and son. Bill Senior was my age or maybe a little older. Bill Junior was in his mid-forties. He obviously loved his father. He was very patient. They had already been on the Trail for over six months. Pickle, Trusty, and Skunk Ape were in their twenties and I would meet up with them shelter after shelter.

I noticed there were ten delicious looking muffins in a box on the table. This was unusual. Once food was put in front of thru-hikers it disappeared fast. I asked: "Does anyone want these muffins?" I got an immediate and unanimous response. "No. No. You go right ahead." It made me suspicious. They were a golden brown. They looked delicious. I picked one up and took a bite. It tasted like cardboard. Where's the sugar? It was dry as a bone. I chewed and chewed. I had just finished hiking 41.1 miles. I needed calories. I ate all ten and drank a lot of water to get them down.

It was 9:00 pm and I hadn't slept for 31 hours. My eyes were heavy. I closed the partition to the smaller room where everyone was watching a documentary on the Appalachian Trail and laughing at it and having a good time. I didn't even know if this was the room we were supposed to sleep in.

I inflated my air mattress, put my blanket liner over it, and slipped into the liner. I remember hearing hikers laughing at the documentary and opening my eyes and it was 7:00 in the morning. I was surrounded by sleeping hikers and the sun was shining through the window.

At this hostel each hiker was assigned a task before they left. Mine was to clean the bathroom sink and mirror. I gave them a good shine. I was the last hiker to leave the hostel. The parishioner whose job it was to further clean the hostel after the hikers left came into the main room. It was so cute. She walked over to the plastic trash can next to the kitchen, opened the lid, and anxiously peered in. The box of muffins was empty. A big smile spread over her face and was still there when I left.

My body hadn't fully recovered from the night hike and for the next few hours I was a weary hiker. Heading up to Prospect Rock, the highest point on the AT in New York, I caught up to Bill Sr. and Bill Jr. We were hiking on a rocky pathway and climbing onto a slippery slab of rock near the top of the mountain. Bill Jr. was leading, Bill Sr. was next, and I was behind Bill Sr. although I couldn't see him. I heard Bill Sr.'s hiking poles slip on the rock surface and heard him fall hard on the rock. I heard his hands and feet gripping frantically to keep from sliding over the side. When I reached him he was sitting on the rock. His hands and knees were bloody and there were a couple of big bumps on his knuckles. He was shaken and should have been. Bill Jr. came running back. "Dad! Are you all right?" "I'm OK, son." That was one lucky man. I don't know how he was able to keep from sliding over the side. He was only about five feet from the edge. The drop-off would either have killed him or broken a lot of bones. He got back to his feet and continued hiking. I followed him. He needed to stop and re-group. He was still shaken.

Later, Bill Jr., I, and a couple of other thru-hikers made it to the Bellville Creamery. The same family had been serving ice cream from this creamery for over fifty years and it was a "go to" place for thru-hikers. Bill Jr. wouldn't order ice cream until his father showed up a half an hour later; then they enjoyed their ice cream together. What a good son. The two Bill's, as everyone called them, made it to Katahdin and had one hell of an adventure along the way. There is a video of them jumping off of a bridge into a river.

After two excellent chocolate malts I headed to Wildcat shelter for the night. Knickers, Hobbit, and her dog Jumar were tented nearby. I didn't see them as much during my hike as I would have liked. We leapfrogged for the rest of the hike and I only talked with them four more times. They summited Katahdin two days before I did. They were in their mid-twenties. This was a hike they had been planning for years. I had the feeling it was a hike of a lifetime for them. Hobbit's husband would sometimes join them. He slack packed them and provided trail magic along the way. They were fast hikers. I knew when they were about to catch up to me. Jumar was always in the lead. I would hear movement behind me and there would be Jumar with his tail wagging, saying: "Hi." Once I acknowledged him he would head back to the sisters. Jumar was a mixed breed. He had a lot of border collie in him. Like all thru-hikers he was rail thin. Hobbit said she didn't know how many times she had answered the question: "He sure is thin. Shouldn't you be giving him more food?" He was loving his thru-hike. There were areas on the Trail that were so challenging that rebar was provided for the hikers. Jumar scampered up those areas unaided. He could even climb ladders. He was a convincing guard dog. If Hobbit and Knickers were camping alone he would challenge anyone coming close to their tents. Once Hobbit said: "It's OK, Jumar." the hackles came down, the barking stopped, and he became a loveable, tail wagging dog waiting to be petted.

The next morning I greeted Jumar as I was heading to the spring to fill my water bottles. He bounded ahead and was slurping thirstily when I arrived. Great. The spring was flowing so I waited a couple of minutes and filled my bottles.

It was a difficult hiking day. I only hiked 14 miles and it took all day to do it. New York didn't have a lot of altitude but there were many difficult climbs and descents. At the end of the day I entered the Lemon Squeezer. The Trail took me between boulders that became narrower as I climbed. Toward the end, my pack was scraping boulders on my left side and right side and I had to push to get through. I was able to make it through without taking my pack off but my pack still has scratches from the Lemon Squeezer.

10 THE RAIN

2009 was a wet hiking year on the Appalachian Trail. Since leaving Johanna and Bob's on June 19th I had seen very little rain. There had been rain at night in the Shenandoahs but I don't remember any rain in West Virginia, Maryland, Pennsylvania, or New Jersey. I felt lucky, particularly not having to deal with the rocks of Pennsylvania in the rain. Ever the optimist I was starting to think my luck would continue all the way to Katahdin. (I hear you chuckling, again.) Wrong! The rain started in earnest on July 19th and continued for two solid weeks. It seemed fitting that of all the thunderstorms I encountered on my thru- hike the thunderstorm on July 19th was the biggest one of all. It ushered in the rains.

I was tented thirty yards from the Fingerboard shelter in a meadow full of thick grass and tall pines. There were five tents close to mine. The sky began to darken. As I put up my tent I made sure it was staked extra tight. The sky grew darker and it turned from warm to chilly. By 8:00 pm there wasn't even a hint of daylight. It must have been a line of thunderstorms because it lasted forever. I could hear the path of the thunder and it was heading in my direction. It was fast moving and in no time was right over me. Frequent flashes of lightning would light up the tent followed immediately by loud thunder. Sometimes the Flash and Boom were almost simultaneous. I felt vulnerable. There was nothing to protect me from being hit by lightning. I remember thinking: "If it's my time, then it's my time." I kept trying to get my muscles to relax but they were wound tight. Fierce wind and rain pounded the tent. The sound it made was Loud. If I had been trying to communicate with someone next to me at that time I would have been yelling to be heard. I kept wondering how much more the tent fabric could take before it split. The tent poles swayed in the heavy gusts.

Tiny mists of water came through the taut fabric of the tent. Thankfully, the tent held up beautifully. During the worst part of the storm I heard loud cursing from one of the hikers in a tarp tent. The next morning when I looked out the tarp tent was flattened. The hiker found refuge in the tent next to his.

The thunderstorm scrubbed the area. Everything was fresh and clean. The sun was shining. The sky was blue. Birds were chirping. The smell of fragrant flowers permeated the air. Beads of moisture glistened from rocks. Intricate spider webs shimmered in the sunlight. Blueberry bushes were in abundance. I would pick blueberries, pop them into my mouth, and be looking for more as I savored their sweet taste.

I'm glad the day started peacefully because it turned out to be a busy, busy, day. After a couple of passing showers in the morning, the rest of the day was warm and sunny. I started climbing Bear Mountain in the early afternoon. When I reached the top I was engulfed in people. The area had some beautiful views but was an obvious tourist destination. I headed down the steep, rocky Trail. This was where I met my first southbound hiker. SOBO's were thru-hikers who started their hike in June and were heading from Maine to Georgia. They picked a terrible month to start their hike. In Maine it rained for 28 straight days in June. Of the 250 SOBO's who started in June, only 35 made it to the Kennebec River crossing, 153 miles to the south. This was according to the guide who paddled me across the Kennebec River in a canoe and kept records of the people that he ferried. He said there were so many ravenous mosquitoes that Deet 100 was useless. All day long, hikers would be combating swarms of mosquitoes. I didn't know what this SOBO had been through or I would have given him more respect. We chatted for a couple of minutes and moved on.

When I reached the bottom of Bear Mountain there was a large pond. A picnic area was next to the pond. This was a Sunday in July and less than forty miles from New York City. It was absolutely wall to wall people. The area teemed with energy. I could see where America was a melting pot for all the people of the world. There were whites, blacks, hispanics, asians, and people of mid-eastern heritage. They were jammed together having their picnics. Each family didn't interact with the families around them; they seemed to pleasantly ignore each other. Kids were playing and laughing. There was a roped off area for swimming. Meat was being barbequed and the smell was wonderful. There were picnic tables filled with chicken, ribs, beef, sausages, potato salad, potato chips, cakes, cookies....my stomach was growling. Across the street from the picnic area was the Bear Mountain Zoo. The Trail passed right through the zoo and was free to thru-hikers. It closed five minutes before I arrived. I was disappointed. I wanted to see the animals, but the two hundred yards of the Trail through the zoo to the Bear Mountain Bridge, was the original Appalachian Trail. This was where the first steps were taken in 1923.

It was after 5:00 pm and I had to re-supply. The grocery store was four miles away. After walking a couple of miles there was a fork in the road. I wasn't sure which way to go so I stopped at a garage to ask directions. The mechanic started giving me directions and said: "Oh hell! It'll be easier to drive you there." So many trail angels.

After I re-supplied I was in the grocery store parking lot organizing my food bag. A nice car pulled up and the driver asked if I needed a ride back to the Trail. I got in. The seat was covered with rich, clean, smooth, (as Ricardo Moltoban used to say with flair), "genuine Corrrrinthian Leather". I was pretty funky but the driver didn't flinch as I sat down. He owned a BBQ restaurant that I passed on my way to the grocery store. It had been packed with customers. He had seen me walk by and gone out of his way to drive to the grocery store, pick me up, and deliver me to the Trail. What can I say?

Even with all this generosity that saved six miles of walking, it was dark by the time I started hiking. I crossed the Hudson River on the Bear Mountain Bridge and entered the forest. There was an immediate steep climb. As I was climbing I could see all the activity along the Hudson River. I listened to lively music and laughter from a night club for the next half hour.

I reached Hemlock Springs campsite at 10:00 pm after a 16 mile day. There were a couple of tents at the campsite and the hikers were asleep so I found a place to put my tent 100 feet from them. I prided myself on my ability to throw a bear bag rope over a high branch. That night I couldn't get the rope over the branch to save my life. I was making enough noise that I could hear people in the tents stirring. Finally I hung my food bag. It was a pleasant night. As I relaxed in my sleeping blanket I listened to firecrackers which I had heard the last couple of hours. It was past the Fourth of July. Then it dawned on me. It was rifle fire. The US Military Academy was nearby and West Point cadets were going through night training.

I slept in for a change and didn't get started until 10:00 am. I hiked in a light drizzle for the first couple of hours. Where the Trail crossed U.S. 9 there was a convenience store. I had three jumbo sized cookies and some coffee. The rain had stopped but it was hot and muggy. This is where I met Strider for the first time. I had been following his shelter journals since the first part of Tennessee. I didn't catch up to him. We had been leapfrogging throughout the hike. I enjoyed talking with him. He was very upbeat. I had been seeing these gigantic boot prints during my hike that day. When I saw Strider, I could see why. He was about seven feet tall. When I stood next to him while we chatted I thought I was going to get a crick in my neck. It was 2:00 pm when I talked to him. We both planned on stopping at the

Shenandoah Tenting area at the end of the day. It was eighteen miles away. This will show you what a fit twenty year old can do. There were many steep climbs and descents. The terrain was never easy. Strider took off ahead of me. Ten minutes later, I followed. I decided to try to keep up with him and started hiking as fast as I could. I didn't let up. I felt like I was moving fast. I was passing other hikers and wasn't being passed. I was starting to run out of daylight and still had a long way to go. My goal was the Shenandoah Tenting area so I kept on hiking in the dark. Pretty soon I was climbing Shenandoah Mountain. It was a long climb. I crossed rock slabs where it was difficult to determine the pathway. I would head in the direction I figured the path should take and move my head left and right until the light from the headlamp spotted the white blaze. I looked at my watch. It was 10:00 pm. Then it was 11:00 pm. I climbed to the top of Shenandoah Mountain and onto a huge slab of rock the size of a basketball court. There was a ten foot by ten foot American flag painted on the rock as a tribute to the victims of 9/11. Unfortunately, there was an empty case of beer with beer cans surrounding it. I stopped for a couple of minutes and turned off my headlamp. It was a beautiful star filled night.

About four hundred yards from the memorial to the 9/11 victims, I found a slab of rock two feet from the Trail. It was flat and just big enough to slide my tent onto. There were bushes on every side but the front. I was tired. I knew if I made it to the Shenandoah Tenting area I would disturb people that late at night. I put up my tent with just the netting, got into my sleeping blanket, and gazed up at ten gillion stars. I was grateful for my air mattress. It kept me from feeling the rock below. I fell asleep easily.

At 1:00 in the morning I heard something moving next to me. I was instantly on full alert! I thought it was a bear. I yelled loudly and aggressively: "HEY! HEY! HEY!" Then I noticed the headlamp light and a man said calmly and pleasantly: "I'm sorry to have disturbed you." He continued down the Trail. That's the first time I met Car Hop. I saw him many more times. We met for the last time twenty miles before Katahdin. It took a few minutes for my heartbeat to get back to normal.

The next morning I saw the most beautiful sunrise of my hike. I was looking up through blueberry bushes at clouds turning delicate shades of red. I unzipped my tent and picked fresh, plump, blueberries without even getting out of my sleeping blanket. Breakfast in bed.

I hiked for another hour and a half before reaching the Shenandoah Tenting area. Strider was packing up and getting ready to leave. He had gotten to the tenting area at 8:00 pm. He averaged over 3 mph in that rocky terrain. Wow! He was so fast he could take time off for a wedding, visit friends in Washington DC, and New York City, and still stay ahead of me. I continued to leapfrog with him all the way to New Hampshire. He summited Katahdin on the 7th of September.

After leaving the Shenandoah Tenting area, I hiked twenty miles in a constant rain; no thunder or lightning, but just a lot of mud, slippery roots, and rocks. I stopped for a lunch break at the deli on N.Y 52 to get out of the rain. From New York all the way to the 100 Mile Wilderness in Maine, I started hitting the deli's. By this time I had almost no body fat. In order to move forward efficiently I needed a lot of calories. There were many deli's less than half a mile off of the Trail. All thru-hikers knew where they were and looked forward to them. I had been frugal as far as spending money on restaurants, motels, and hostels up until New York. From New York on, I didn't hold back on the deli's and restaurants. I still enjoyed my trail mix, but I was tired of the ramen noodles, rice dishes, pastas, peanut butter, and tuna packets. There was nothing like a big grinder. The bun was like a Subway foot long and I could choose any meats I wanted, with lettuce, tomatoes, cheese, mayo, and anything else that looked good. I would usually eat two grinders and two potato salads with a coke. I would keep adding food until I was completely full. Deli's were great morale boosters.

When I arrived at Telephone Pioneers shelter that evening, Pickle, Trusty, Skunk Ape, Hobbit, Knickers, and Jumar, were there. A trail maintainer brought a couple of six packs of beer and was visiting before heading back to his car. The beer tasted good at the end of the day. He had a lively pup who wanted to play with Jumar. Jumar had hiked over 1,400 miles with a good sized pack and he would have none of it. He retreated to the back of the shelter, curled up, and growled a couple of times when the pup tried to visit.

I didn't know it at the time, but, like me, Pickle, Trusty, and Skunk Ape were trying to average eighteen miles a day. I bumped into them either hiking, or at a shelter, time after time. They were a very tight knit group. All were in their twenties. Pickle and Trusty met within a couple of days of starting the Trail in Georgia. Skunk Ape joined their group within a week.

Pickle was goal oriented and disciplined. Once she set her goal, she zeroed in on it with a laser like focus.

By the time I met Trusty he had lost fifty pounds. You would never have known he had been overweight. He looked like the typical, skinny hiker with the big beard. He worked well with Pickle and often I would hear them discussing their plans for the next day. They were both meticulous planners and enjoyed those discussions. I asked them when they planned to summit Katahdin. Their answer was immediate and simultaneous - September 12th. Of course, they did.

Skunk Ape was incredibly fit. He was so much faster than Pickle and Trusty, who were no slouches themselves; that he frequently slept until 10:00 or later each morning. He hardly ever hiked with Pickle and Trusty. They stayed in touch by cell phone and would figure out where to meet each night. Sometimes cell phone batteries would run low or there were areas with no reception in the mountains and Skunk Ape would become separated from the group. This caused Pickle and Trusty all kinds of anxiety. They would try to communicate with Skunk Ape through the shelter journals: "Where are you Skunky?"

Skunk Ape was one of the fastest hikers on the Trail. In areas I couldn't come close to averaging 2 mph, Skunk Ape could average 3 mph. Hiking those nasty rocks at that speed had to have pounded his and other young bodies. It takes over 5,000,000 steps to hike the 2,178 mile Appalachian Trail. I always wondered if they were going to pay the price later in life. Skunk Ape planned to meet his family on the 5th of September at Katahdin. Eventually he had to part with Pickle and Trusty. That was such a tight group it must have been a tearful departure.

A thunderstorm came through in the night. It rained throughout the night and all the next day. It was a dark, dreary day; a perfect day for making miles. I couldn't take breaks between shelters or I would get cold and my trail mix would get soggy, so I hiked non-stop from shelter to shelter.

I crossed into Connecticut and stopped at the Mt. Algo lean-to after a 21 mile day. Shelters were called lean-to's in Connecticut. With so much continuous rain, the ground became saturated and the mud puddles deepened. Sometimes trail maintainers put wooden planks over muddy, swampy, parts of the Trail. Each plank was about ten feet long and a foot wide and was anchored by a thick four foot log at each end. There were usually two planks side by side so that each boot was on a plank as you walked over them. Some planks were loose or rotten and they were slick when they were wet. This was another time when hiking poles were worth their weight in gold. Planks could be strung together for two hundred yards or more. Usually, they covered muddy areas that were permanently in shade and wouldn't dry.

If there wasn't planking, you often had to get creative going over muddy areas. Trail maintainers sometimes strategically placed rocks in muddy areas. Using your hiking poles for balance you could hop from one to the next. You also could step on dead branches or pieces of wood to try to skirt around the mud. Sometimes it wouldn't be as dry as it looked and you would sink as far as your knee in the mud. Talk about colorful cussing. I would quietly chuckle when I heard it from other hikers. (Been there. Done that.) Hikers made new trail around the muck. That was destructive to the Trail but there were times when I used it.

In the afternoon the wind picked up and the rain intensified. The streams were swollen and at times the water would be over my knees as I was crossing. My shoes were totally soaked so I would cross a stream without taking them off. I never could understand how people could walk across a stream barefoot. I needed the stability of my shoes. Entering the stream, the cold water was a jolt to my system. I felt the smooth, slick, mossy, rocks, and using my hiking poles as stabilizers, focused on not letting the swiftly moving water push me over.

The Trail had turned into a stream. Areas that were flat became pools of water and mud. After a while my boots, socks, and legs were so covered with mud that it didn't matter any more. I stopped hopping from rock to rock and headed in a straight line. Walking through the thick mud puddles, I didn't know if my next step was going to be up to my knee. Frequently it was over my ankle and I could feel the mud trying to pull my shoe off.

All of a sudden I was having fun! For the next couple of hours I picked the muckiest, nastiest, mud and headed right through it. I would stomp down hard and watch the mud and water explode in all directions. I was a nine year old again and loving it!

I ran out of daylight before I made it to the next shelter. The shelter was full. I found a spot to put my tent thirty yards uphill from the shelter. There was thunder and lightning and a lot of wind when I started to set up my tent. Heavy raindrops were splashing little pieces of mud onto my legs. The tent was flapping energetically in the wind as I was trying to put in the tent poles. I couldn't shield the interior of the tent from the intense rain and it was getting soaked. My clothes were soaked. My legs were caked with mud. I was filthy. Unless I was hit by lightning it couldn't have gotten any worse. It was so absurd, it became funny!

I started laughing and singing: "Singing In The Rain. Just Singing In The Rain… FLASH! BOOM!… What A Glorious Feeling. I'm Happy Again." I even did a little Gene Kelly soft shoe in the mud. There was absolutely no reason why I should have been, but I WAS happy.

When I woke the next morning there was a puddle of water next to my feet. The sleeping blanket had overlapped my air mattress and was wet. I had curled up my feet in the night to stay away from the wet area. Fortunately, Kent, Connecticut was only two miles away. The first thing I did was go to the Laundromat. All of my clothes and socks were wet and muddy. My sleeping blanket was wet and smelly. I put on my sleeping shorts and put everything else into the wash. I took a sponge bath in the restroom. I even used my Dr. Bonner's Soap. I left the restroom cleaner than I found it.

I was shirtless, barefoot, and chatting with a couple of other thru-hikers who were the same. The owner of the establishment came in red faced and furious:

"Didn't you read the sign for hikers on the front door?"

"No. Sorry."

"All you hikers think you can take over this place! You use the bathroom to wash yourselves and leave it filthy! You walk around half naked! My regular customers don't want to see that! You can't walk around here barefoot! You're supposed to put your packs out in back! You can't leave them in front of the Laundromat!"

Yikes! Despite the harsh treatment, when I left, it felt good to have clean socks, clean shorts, and a clean shirt, covering my clean body.

I re-supplied at the grocery store and headed to the outfitters. I bought another pair of socks. I went through seven pair of socks on my hike. At the beginning of my thru-hike if I got a pebble in my shoe I would stop, take the shoe off, and take out the pebble. That was time consuming. An experienced thru-hiker told me he just let pebbles collect in his shoes. He said he could feel them roll around the interior of his shoe but that eventually the bottom of his feet became so hardened they would pulverize the little pebbles and he never had to take his shoes off during a hike. That sounded interesting so I tried it. I would feel the pebble working its way around the bottom of my foot. A lot of the time it would end up in front of my toes and wouldn't be a bother. As the bottom of my feet became tougher, I could feel the little pebbles begin to disintegrate as I was hiking. The soles of my feet became as tough as leather. Unfortunately, the little pebbles did a job on my socks.

I bought a new pair of boots - Merrell Vibram's. The trail runners I bought in Waynesboro, Virginia were completely shot. Big chunks of the sole were gone; enough to affect my stride. There were holes in the mesh, and the rubber flap that covered the toe was loose on both shoes.

I don't know why I didn't use common sense when it came to replacing my hiking shoes. They were shot by the time I was finished with the rocks of Pennsylvania. It had taken twenty-four days from the time I left my sister's to my last day in Pennsylvania. My thrifty little mind said that $95 trail runners should last more than twenty-four days. I had not gotten my money's worth from those shoes. I needed to get my money's worth. After leaving Pennsylvania, for the next 172 miles I continued pulling off pieces of rubber from the sole of both shoes until I reached Kent, Connecticut. The pads of my feet became puffier and puffier.

The trail runners were designed for speed. The Merrell Vibram's were soft, puffy, and well cushioned. Aaaahhh. What a difference. They didn't grip rock very well on down hills. I would watch hikers ahead of me walk down a rock surface and my boots would slip on the same surface, but my sad little feet loved them!

After leaving the outfitters, I saw a hot dog stand down the street. I had four hot dogs, two potato cakes, and a coke. I passed an ice cream shop and couldn't resist. They advertised a malt zinger with a double shot of espresso. It was great! I was wired for the next four hours. On the way out of town, I passed the Laundromat. I could hear the owner giving a new group of hikers a hard time. Geez! She missed her calling - Drill Sergeant!

I left the pretty little town of Kent, Connecticut and headed back into the woods. I met a talkative hiker that I hiked with until we hit the St. John Ledges. This man had cut his section hike short and was trying to get back to his car. He was in his sixties and had a hip replacement the year before. He was way overweight and tired. His limp was painful to watch. St. John Ledges was a steep downhill with boulders and jumbled rocks. There were sheer drop-offs. I had to slowly pick my way down, often stretching to my limit, from rock to rock. This guy was having a hard enough time on the regular Trail. When he started the Ledges, he looked like a disaster ready to happen. It took me a half an hour getting down the Ledges and I headed to the shelter three miles away. One person was at the shelter and he had been hiking with the other man earlier. We both anxiously waited for him to arrive. We waited for an hour, then two hours. I was getting ready to go back to look for him. Two section hikers arrived at the shelter with a message from the man. He made it to the bottom of the Ledges but was out of energy and had found a camping spot. That was a relief. I put up my tent in an area next to the Housatonic River. I was under tall trees and by a clean rapidly flowing brook that I used to fill my water bottles.

I walked along this beautiful river for three miles the next morning. The pathway had been used for many years. The surrounding forest with its thick trees had once been farmland. I followed old moss covered rock walls for miles. A couple of hundred years ago farmers cleared their fields of rocks and used the rocks to build walls to mark their boundaries. A lot of the walls were three feet thick and three to five feet high. It was interesting to see the differences in craftsmanship. Some walls were beautifully crafted with tightly placed rocks while others were pretty sloppy. The craftsmanship probably reflected the Felixes and Oscars of the early farmers.

As I walked along the Housatonic River I spent a good deal of time slapping mosquitoes. I'm sure there had been mosquitoes from the beginning. Connecticut was the first state I remember them bothering me. There were so many of them! I spent hour after hour listening to their constant buzzing as they circled my body. I would feel the little pin prick of a mosquito getting ready to draw blood and quickly brush it away; time after countless time. Deet would last about an hour. I used a lot. It was summer and I was usually sweating profusely. I could tell when the effect of the Deet was wearing off. More mosquitoes would surround me and become bolder. Instead of just circling, they would occasionally land. Then more and more would land. I had to keep moving as I took off my pack to get out the Deet, otherwise I would have many biting me at the same time. Once I put the Deet on it was like night and day. The mosquitoes would circle and come in for a landing - and not land. For an hour I would be mosquito free. The mosquitoes were annoying in Connecticut. After days of rain and one of the wettest summers in Massachusetts history they were unbelievable in Massachusetts and stayed that way through the first part of Vermont. From then on they were mostly annoying. When I entered Connecticut, I was carrying three bottles of Deet 100. I went through them in no time. Hikers were always talking about getting cancer from Deet 100. I didn't care. To me, it was worth the risk just to have those mosquitoes off of me for a while.

The mosquitoes in Connecticut, Massachusetts, and Vermont, drove people in the shelters crazy. They had to contend with the buzzing and biting all night long. I think that is one of the reasons so many people left the Trail in those states. At night someone would always start a fire if it wasn't raining hard. Mosquitoes would be buzzing around. Once the fire started to blaze they would leave. I really appreciated my tent. When I was ready to enter the tent for the night, I would quickly unzip it, slide in, and quickly zip it up. I would watch all the mosquitoes buzzing around the netting trying to get it. It was very satisfying.

That was a lot more about mosquitoes than I expected to write. They earned their due.

After an enjoyable walk along the river, I headed into the mountains. An hour into the hike I was passed by Joe Kick Ass.

"Wingo, there's a bunch of Cub Scouts about five minutes behind you."

Great! The ultimate humiliation! Being passed by Cub Scouts! Would that be my legacy?

"Wingo? Isn't that the guy who was passed by the Cub Scouts?"

"Yea. Poor guy."

I wasn't going to have some little pip-squeak Cub Scout say: "Have a good day, mithtur." as he passed me on the Trail. No sir! No sir! I picked up my pace. In fact, I hiked like the wind! Well, sort of: "Oof! Ouch! Damned rocks! Ouch. I'm getting too old for this! Ouch!"

I'm proud to report that I left the Cub Scouts in the dust.

This turned into a long 22 mile day. I stopped at Limestone Spring lean-to. It was one of the most beautiful locations of all. It was starting to get dark when I left the Trail and headed the half mile down to the lean-to. One area along the pathway had a steep drop-off to a swiftly moving stream. The trail was not well marked. I couldn't believe the trail would go down the side of that steep drop-off. I searched for alternatives. They all led back to the steep trail. I didn't want to risk it in the dark and was ready to head back to the main Trail when Slapshot approached. He did the same as me and looked for alternative paths. When he came to the same conclusion, he headed down the precarious pathway - effortlessly. It was extremely steep with loose footing. It was almost dark and he didn't have his headlamp on. I followed as best I could but soon he was out of sight.

I saw Slapshot hiking in Vermont and the White Mountains in New Hampshire. He was a mountain goat! There was no one who could scamper up a mountain faster or more effortlessly than Slapshot. It was fun watching the best. It was like watching Roger Federer play tennis. I would watch him scramble up practically a vertical wall of rock with my mouth open and shake my head in amazement. "How did he do that?" He seemed to instinctively know where to find the right foot and handholds without breaking his momentum. I didn't have much time to watch him. He averaged 3 mph on even the toughest climbs. I saw him on a number of occasions because like most twenty-three year olds he went to weddings, visited friends off Trail, and knew where the parties were. He could have hiked the Trail in under three months if that had been his goal. He summited Katahdin on the 12th of September.

When I finally made it to Limestone Spring lean-to it was dark. Pickle and Trusty were there. We had leap-frogged most of the day. I had my dinner in the shelter and then found a beautiful, flat area twenty yards in front of the shelter, for my tent. Halfway into putting up my tent it started to rain lightly. I quickly covered the netting so the interior stayed dry, staked down the tent, and hopped inside. Just in time. An intense thunderstorm came through and after it passed it continued to rain the rest of the night. I loved listening to the soothing patter of rain on my tent. It made me feel secure and appreciate that I wasn't out in it. It usually put me quickly to sleep.

Since I had gotten in late and hiked over twenty miles, I slept in the next morning. It was such a beautiful location it lured me into taking my time and enjoying it. Limestone Springs lean-to was difficult to get to, almost dangerous in my opinion, but the people who created the Appalachian Trail couldn't resist this beautiful area. It was in a small canyon between two lovely streams. It was under tall pine trees in an area filled with lush vegetation and interesting rock formations.

There was a limestone spring with cool, clear water that was my favorite spring of all. The water was wonderful. I loved water that was just the right cool temperature, perfectly clear, and had absolutely no taste. Since I didn't filter my water I became very knowledgeable about water. I tasted water from streams, brooks, seeps, springs, wells, and runoff from shelter roofs. I drank water that was slightly yellow, slightly brown, had little particles in it, and a slight odor to it. I didn't want a swift flow of water that would churn up particles. I looked for smooth flowing water. If the flow was too slow or stagnant I passed. Most shelters were located next to good water, although not all of them. Ideally, I would find a stream or spring high in the mountains with a smooth flow of water. I was particular about the water I drank. There were times when I was very thirsty and passed on water that didn't look good enough. I used Aqua Mira tablets three times and threw them away. My stomach didn't feel quite right after purifying the water with the tablets. Maybe I was lucky. I dipped my water bottles into a couple of hundred streams and springs. Probably I was lucky. A number of people I hiked with who purified their water contracted giardia. They were only too happy to tell about their bodily functions when they had giardia. I will spare you the details.

Leaving Limestone Spring lean-to I hiked three miles to U.S. 44 and a re-supply in Salisbury, Connecticut. It threatened to rain while I was in town but waited until I was back on the Trail. The climb up to Lion's Head wasn't too difficult. The climb up Bear Mountain was more challenging. The descent into Sages Ravine was rocky, steep, and very challenging. I tossed my hiking poles down to a lower level quite a few times and used my hands descending from rock to rock. I was passed by a couple of kids in their early teens who were making quick work of the descent. Pretty soon the father passed me. He was exhausted. He was trying to catch up to his son and his son's friend. He was so tired he was making mistakes. He barely saved himself from falls a couple of times. I passed them at the bottom of the ravine when they were taking a break. The Trail followed a beautiful little stream. The kids passed me and eventually the father passed me. He was so tired he could barely pick up his feet and was constantly stumbling. We all headed up to the Sages Brook Ravine Campsite. It was a steep trail. The kids were leading and I was right behind the father. By now he was shuffling along. He would take a step forward with his heavy pack and teeter backwards. I put my hands out a couple of times when I thought he was going to topple over but he managed to stay upright. It was painful to hear the ragged inhale and exhale of his lungs. He didn't have enough common sense to slow down. His son was embarrassed by his lack of conditioning. "C'mon, Dad. Hurry up!" He was a heart attack waiting to happen but he was giving it his all!

This was another great campsite, almost as beautiful as Limestone Springs. I placed my tent over a soft, fragrant matting of pine needles. It was a spacious campground so I didn't have to worry about disturbing my neighbors. A brief thunderstorm passed through then I slept soundly.

The moist air from the rains the night before left the surrounding valleys in fog. Immediately after leaving Sages Brook Ravine campsite I was into a thousand foot climb up Race Mountain. I was climbing in fog and broke out of the fog near the top. For far as I could see in any direction there was an even layer of fog below me. It looked like snow covered ground. The sun was reflecting off of it and the light was intense. The sky was a bright, deep blue. Distant mountain peaks reached through the fog like tiny islands. For two miles I walked along the ridgeline on slabs of rock just a few feet above the fog. Sometimes the fog would drift toward me. The surrounding temperature immediately became cooler. I could feel the wisp of breeze as it touched me and feel tiny moisture particles on my skin. I continued on and eventually climbed to the top of Mt. Everett. The fog began to break up and I saw patches of farmland in the valley below. Descending Mt. Everett, almost all of the pathway was muddy. The mud thickened on the bottom of my shoes. I had very little traction and was relying heavily on my hiking poles. It made for a tricky, slippery descent. At the bottom of Mt. Everett, I crossed the field where Shay's Rebellion had taken place. There was a monument marking the spot.

It was 8:30 pm by the time I reached the Tom Leonard Lean-to. Everyone was in bed. I couldn't find a level spot in the dark to put my tent. The lean-to was a spacious double-decker so I decided to stay there. The people were asleep, so as quietly as I could, I hoisted my pack to the second level and got into my sleeping bag. I wondered why this group was in bed at 8:30 pm and had so obviously been asleep before I got there. The next morning I checked my watch with one of the hikers. Oops. My watch had been soaked too many times in the last few days and was an hour off. I had gotten there at 9:30 the previous night. The people in this shelter were hiking as a group. There were six of them. They all acted tired and lethargic. I would hear deep sighs. Most of them were still sound asleep when I left the shelter at 9:00 am.

11 UPPER GOOSE POND CABIN

My destination was Upper Goose Pond Cabin. This was a place all thru-hikers looked forward to. The pond was large and in a beautiful location. There was a canoe available for hikers. The cabin could accommodate twenty hikers. There were bunk beds with soft mattresses, a living room, and a screened in porch. There were free blueberry pancakes for breakfast.

I had to hike 21 miles through miserable conditions to get there. This was in Massachusetts. It had been raining continuously for a week. The ground was completely saturated. Little streams on the sides of mountains were now big streams. Water was flowing down the slopes everywhere. It wasn't even trying to find streams to follow. The Trail at times became a rapidly flowing stream. When I was climbing on this Trail I was fighting the current or hopping rock to rock to stay out of the current. Descents were tricky. The rocks were slick. The Trail was often steep. The flow of the downward rushing water was enough to throw me off balance. I would plant my hiking poles and make sure they were secure before descending. There was mud everywhere. Pools of water were everywhere. They became breeding grounds for mosquitoes. I have never in my life been around so many mosquitoes. About halfway through the day I did a 'face plant'. I was heading through a big wide mud bog. There were small tree branches stuck in the mud. I was maneuvering over the branches when the hiking pole in my right hand got caught in one of the branches. The hiking pole in my left hand was behind me. I stumbled into the branch and started falling forward. I couldn't get the hiking pole in my right hand out of the branch fast enough to plant it for support and fell down face first in the mud. My left hand broke the fall but not enough to keep my face out of the mud. I had mud all over my face, cap, shirt, shorts, and legs. Mud was in my mouth and I could feel its gravelly texture and earthy taste before I spit it out. The first thing I did was get up quickly and look around to see if anyone had seen me fall. Nobody had. Whew! When I reached the next stream, I washed off the mud and continued on. That was a shock to have my face flat in the mud.

I made it to Upper Goose Pond Cabin just before dark. After I closed the door to the screened porch the skies opened up and it poured. I was complimented on my good timing. The place was crowded with thru-hikers, many that I had not seen before. There was a long picnic table on the screened in porch. People had their stoves out and were making dinner. Others were in the living room sitting on a soft sofa and soft chairs and chatting. After sitting on benches, rocks, and hard shelter floors; soft chairs and a soft sofa were a luxury. I made my dinner and visited. The people at Upper Goose Pond Cabin had hiked over 1,538 miles and had a common interest in hiking. It was a convivial group and I enjoyed being part of it.

There were two brothers making their dinner across the table from me. This was the only time I saw them. Corporate was the trail name of one of the brothers, I don't remember the other brother's name. They were around nineteen and twenty years old. They were trying to hike the Appalachian Trail in less than ninety days. To put the speed of their hike in perspective: It was July 28th. We were at Upper Goose Pond Cabin, 1,538 miles into our journey. We had 640 miles to go. I was hiking a fast thru-hike. I had been on the Trail exactly 90 days.

They were averaging over 25 miles a day which included re-supply days. They had many 30 plus mile days. They hadn't taken any days off. This far into my hike I realized how hard it was to maintain a high daily mileage. I had a lot of questions:

"How many hours a day do you hike?" [We don't put in more hours than most people. We start at 9:00 am and finish before dark.]

"Do you take breaks?   [We take a fifteen minute break every two hours.]

"How do you make so many miles?   [We hike fast. Our packs weigh less than fourteen pounds with food and water.]

"How do you get the weight down to 14 pounds?   [We only stay at shelters. We don't have a tent. If a shelter is full, we have a ground cloth to cover us for the night. We carry light weight dehydrated food on the Trail and find all-you-can-eat restaurants when we re-supply.]

Watching them was like watching little hummingbirds. The whole time I was there they were feeding their high metabolisms. Their movements were quick and their speech patterns were rapid.

A lot of the other hikers couldn't understand why they would want to go that fast and have less of the social experience. I had nothing but admiration for them. They hiked the Appalachian Trail in 96 days.

All the bunks were taken. I was eating my dinner slowly hoping the rain would stop. Soon it was completely dark and still raining. Reluctantly I headed out to find a place to put my tent. This was a heavily used, ecologically fragile area, so tent platforms were being used. This was the first time I used these platforms. I used them probably ten more times the rest of my hike. I disliked them at first and would always much rather put my tent on the ground, but I adapted and by Maine was able to set up a fairly tight tent on the platform.

If someone says Massachusetts, my immediate response would be: rain, mud, and mosquitoes. Unfortunately, that's how I remember it. The next day was more of the same. I climbed Beckett Mountain and Bald Top before finally reaching the Kay Wood lean-to. I hiked 19 miles and was proud of it. It was pouring rain when I got there. Two women in the upper loft were already in their sleeping bags and looked exhausted. On the lower level was a section hiker who I talked with for the next two hours as I made dinner and prepared for bed.

I liked talking with enthusiastic section hikers. The section hiker at the Kay Wood lean-to was eager to be talking with a thru-hiker. He was a wonderful listener. He was genuinely interested in what I had to say and I found myself talking a lot more about my hike than I normally did. I would tell of one of my adventures and when I finished his next question would be: "And then what?" Woah. I wasn't used to that. Talking with other thru-hikers around the campfire, they would be good listeners when you were telling your story, but when you finished they were anxious to jump in and tell of an adventure of their own. He was in his early fifties. I could tell that he, like so many other hikers I talked to, would have given anything to be able to hike the Appalachian Trail in one continuous year but because of health, family, work, or other reasons, was not able to do it. He was vicariously hiking the Appalachian Trail through me. It was a pleasure talking with him.

This was the last shelter I slept in. Shelters were wonderful places for getting out of the wind or cold. They were much appreciated for their cover during a rain. I enjoyed going to the shelter at the end of the day, making dinner, and socializing. I disliked sleeping in them. Usually they were dirty. I always took a broom provided by the shelter and swept the area where I was going to sleep. You couldn't get away from the mosquitoes. When I would hear a mosquito buzzing I would cover my head with my sleeping blanket. If it was a warm night, that didn't last long. Parts of the night would be spent trying to keep from being bitten. The no-see-ums used to drive me crazy. They would make me itch. I would scratch my scalp, arms, chest, and shoulders, almost continuously. At some shelters I wasn't bothered by no-see-ums and at others it was non-stop scratching.

They almost always had mice. The mice came out at night. I would hear them running along the ceiling rafters; then they would get bolder and scamper across the shelter floor. If someone was dumb enough to leave their pack on the floor they would go after that. Some mice were aggressive and would try to get into my sleeping blanket. When that happened I would cover the blanket around my head and close any openings. I knew that the mouse that had tried to get into my sleeping blanket would do the same with other sleeping bags. It never failed. Within minutes someone would be jumping out of their sleeping bag and cursing.

Thin, sturdy, pieces of rope were hung from ceiling beams. At the bottom of each rope was a three inch piece of wood that hooked onto the loop on the back of a backpack. Tied near the top of the rope was the bottom section of a tuna, coke, or beer can. This kept mice from traveling down the rope to the pack. After spending many nights in a shelter I got used to the mice. I might feel one scamper over my sleeping blanket or brush my head on its way by but I would close my eyes and go back to sleep.

I never could get used to being around so many people at night. There were always loud snorers. After hiking eight or more hours most hikers were only too ready to go to bed. Nine p.m., or Hiker Midnight, was when they turned off their headlamps and went to sleep. There were always a couple of "night people" who continued talking around the campfire until 10:00 or 11:00 pm. Throughout the night, people were getting up and heading outside. I stopped my fluid intake by 6:00 pm but there were hot days where I had to stay hydrated to the end of my hike and I would be one of the people getting up two or more times in the night.

Many times the shelters were full. That meant having your sleeping bag within a foot of the person on either side of you. Some hikers smelled awful even by hiker's standards and you would be trying to find ways not to inhale that odor for most of the night. Being that close to your neighbor, you could hear every movement. I worried about bothering other people. All of my life I have been a restless sleeper. When I moved, my sleeping blanket would rub against the fabric of the air mattress and it made a lot of noise. I would try to stay still but it threw off my normal sleep routine and was annoying. Starting in Virginia, whenever I put in high mileage days, once or twice a minute my left leg would involuntarily kick. That made a lot of noise. I was always a light sleeper when I slept in shelters and even a fart would wake me up. There were plenty of those.

I put my tent up near shelters. I would stay far enough away so that I wasn't distracted by the noise from the shelter. There was a feeling of security being close to shelters at night and I enjoyed socializing at the shelters at the end of the day.

I left the Kay Wood lean-to the next morning and hiked three miles through the muck to Dalton, Massachusetts. The Trail went right through the small town of Dalton. I stopped at the Laundromat. It had been almost a week since I had cleaned my clothes in Kent, Connecticut. I had hiked through a lot of rain and mud. My shoes and socks were caked with mud and smelled atrocious. My clothes and body didn't smell much better. While my clothes were being washed, I sprayed my shoes with the outside hose and got them as clean as I could. I went back into the Laundromat barefoot and headed to the bathroom. I used the Dr. Bonner's soap and cleaned up. I left the bathroom as spotless as I found it. After the Kent, Connecticut Laundromat incident, I was a little apprehensive when I left the bathroom and walked past the owner. He was nothing but kind. He even asked a couple of questions about my hike.

Near the Laundromat was a small grocery store with a deli. They made their own bread and the aroma of freshly baked bread was intoxicating. I had a turkey grinder, a roast beef grinder, and left happy. The Trail continued through the residential section of Dalton for another mile. People were going about their everyday activities; mowing lawns, working in gardens, chatting with neighbors. Dalton was a friendly town. One lady even came out of her house and cheerfully pointed me back in the right direction when I missed the turnoff to the Trail. She had a glass of iced tea in her hand with beads of moisture rolling down the side. It looked cold and delicious. I think if I had stared at it long enough she might have gotten the hint, but I didn't push my luck.

I passed through Dalton and the Trail climbed to Gore Pond. It was in a rustic area, almost swampy, with swarms of mosquitoes. There was a beaver dam that would have been fun to explore but I needed to be moving because of the mosquitoes.

Four hours later I made it to the Mark Noepel lean-to in a ferocious thunderstorm. I was the first person there. I was followed by Ferdie and Schooner. They were a nice young couple that I would see off and on up to New Hampshire. Ferdie could have been a model. She had a beautiful, sculpted, almost angelic face. She was spitting mad. I didn't know rain could be described in such colorful terms. Schooner and I couldn't have agreed more and were enjoying her tirade. She had been hiking in a thunderstorm and was using Trail language to describe the emotions of the moment. Once she got the anger out of her system, she was fine.

Within the hour the shelter was full. This group was mainly in their twenties. I talked with my second SOBO at this lean-to. He was quiet at first, almost taciturn. He was in his forties. He eventually loosened up and was one of the best conversationalists that I met. He made himself sound like a glorified bum at first. He was a Liberal with a capital L. He practiced what he preached. He never owned a car because they polluted the atmosphere. He bicycled everywhere. The year before he had crossed the country on his bicycle. It sounded like he had been going from adventure to adventure for years. He was extremely intelligent and applied his intelligence to his hike. Since he was hiking from north to south, he filled us in on which restaurants to go to and the names of the people to talk to in the restaurants, which hostels to stay at, including places that were not listed as hostels but would let hikers stay overnight, all the deli's not listed in the Guidebook, even a yellow bus parked just off the Trail where you could get hot dogs and ice cream.

He had charisma. It was fascinating to watch how after only a couple of hours he controlled this group of hikers. If they defied or challenged his liberal views he would verbally beat them. He taught at a university in the South three months of the year and made it sound like he had an enthusiastic student following. I'll bet he did. Formidable and mesmerizing would be two words to describe him.

The rain was pouring down the roof of the shelter. Everyone put their water bottles on a picnic table where the runoff from the roof filled them within minutes. The water had no residue, was cool, and had no taste.

When I stopped at the shelter, I only planned to take a break from the rain, eat some trail mix, and head back out. While I was taking my break a violent thunderstorm came through. For the first time in 1,572 miles of hiking I didn't go back into the rain after a break when I had a lot of daylight left. I felt like I had to justify it at first but I was only fourteen miles from Vermont and knew that from here to Katahdin I could coast and still make it in plenty of time. It was a good feeling.

Soon the shelter was packed. At 6:00 pm there was a lull in the rain and I quickly headed to a tent platform fifty yards away and set up my tent. It rained the rest of the night and I slept soundly.

From the Mark Neopol lean-to I climbed up Mount Graylock the next morning. There were mud puddles everywhere. Branches and foliage were saturated with water and soaked the back of my neck when I brushed by them. Bascom Lodge was at the top of Mount Graylock and had recently been renovated. It was within days of re-opening. The dining room was open and I had a cup of hot chocolate. This was my idea of what a lodge should be. It was built of stone. It had beautiful views of the surrounding countryside, particularly from the spacious dining room with its huge fireplace and abundant windows.

On top of Mount Graylock was a tall stone tower with a globe that was lit at night. This mountain was supposed to have been an inspiration for Hawthorne and Thoreau and there were little plaques with Thoreau's writings on them.

It started to rain on the descent from Mount Graylock. In places it was steep and slippery. I passed a swamp that was so full from the rains, it was overflowing. The water was yellowish and smelled swampy.

In the afternoon I made it to Williamstown, Massachusetts. I needed to re-supply and found a good grocery store. When I finished re-supplying, it was raining heavily. The Redwood Motel was across the street. My Thru-Hikers' Companion Guidebook listed it as being $70 a night. I was tempted to head back to the Trail. It was raining damned hard though. Indecision. Indecision. I finally decided to spend the $70 and headed across the street. Since it was raining, I left my pack outside and went into the motel's office. No one was there but someone started talking to me:

"There is a camera above you and to the left. Look at it. Do you want a room?"

"Yes. I would like a single. How much is it?"

"Are you going to pay cash or credit card?"

Hmmrn. This man wants to negotiate. The motel is empty. Why not?

"Cash."

"On weekends we charge $85 and up a night." (It was Thursday - July 30th.)

"Sorry. That's more than I can pay. I can pay $60, though."

"$60 plus tax."

"OK."

"The motel manager is cleaning Room 12. I will ring him and he will be right over."

"OK."

It turned out to be a nice, clean motel. I took a long, hot shower. I went back across the street to the grocery store. They had an excellent deli. I bought two grinders, potato salad, macaroni salad, and stuffed myself when I returned to my room. The rain continued to pour. I opened my curtain and watched it pounding on the parking lot and was pleased with my decision to get a room. The soft bed and clean sheets felt good, too.

The next morning, I headed to the grocery store and hit the bakery. I headed back to my motel room with sweet rolls, cinnamon rolls, and some excellent coffee. I was riding a sugar high when I started my hike. It was raining heavily when I headed out of town but I felt good.

12 VERMONT

It rained all day. I spent most of the day grinding through mud and more mud with a heavy dose of mosquitoes. I passed from Massachusetts into Vermont. Vermud to be more accurate. At the state border the Appalachian Trail joined the Long Trail. The Long Trail was a very popular trail and older than the Appalachian Trail. The combination of the two trails showed in the amount of wear. It was one big, wide, sloppy, slippery, mud bog.

I hiked into darkness to get to the Congdon shelter. It was packed, of course. I took a short break at the shelter before I set up my tent. The shelter was built for eight people. There were at least ten. The attitude of the hikers was negative. One of the hikers went off on a tirade about how bad things were on the Trail and it felt like everybody was giving him encouragement. Misery loves company. It had been raining constantly for days. There was a powerful stench in the shelter from dirty boots, socks, clothes, and bodies. It was almost overpowering. This shelter journal and other shelter journals echoed hiker's feelings: "This fuckin' never-ending rain!!!" "This fuckin' mud!!!" "These fuckin' mosquitoes!!!!!

Many hikers quit during this period of constant rain. Everyone had a legitimate cause to complain, when it became whiny, I got away from that person or group. Thinking back, I didn't hike with anyone. I mainly socialized with people during breaks and occasionally at the end of the day.

It was a trying time, though. After days of rain, everything was wet. Everything inside my backpack was covered by a thick 30 gallon garbage bag but there was so much moisture that I couldn't control it. My tent never leaked but there was a lot of condensation that dripped onto my sleeping blanket, air mattress, and tent floor. After a while they had a musty smell.

Once I got into my sleeping blanket at night it took a while to get used to the odor. I wore the same damp shorts and damp shirt I had been hiking in. (My camp clothes were so funky it wasn't worth changing.) It was chilly at night so I would put my head into the sleeping blanket and could smell the musty air mattress and the musty sleeping blanket. My nose would be next to my shirt which had the sour smell of Deet 100 and many days of sweat. I could smell my own foul body odor. I longed for a sunny day where I could spread out my tent, sleeping blanket, and air mattress, and let them dry.

In these wet conditions it was essential that I take care of my feet. I had a routine I followed each night. I would take off my boots and step into the tent. I would take off my filthy socks and holding them outside the tent, would rub them together to loosen the caked on mud and sand. Back inside the tent, I would use my fingernails to loosen any stubborn dirt on the outside of the sock. I would turn the sock inside out and shake the sand loose. I then took my sham wow cloth, poured water on it, and thoroughly cleaned my feet and legs.

If there were any blisters or hot spots, I covered them with duct tape. When this was done, I put my camp socks on. Just doing this minor cleaning helped save my feet from blisters. The soles of my feet were tough from 1,500 miles of hiking but the mud and sand that accumulated in my socks and boots during a day's hike wouldn't allow for a smooth fit with the insoles of my boots. I used a lot of duct tape covering hot spots on my heels, toes, and the pad next to my toes. Even reliable duct tape only stuck for a day or two. Band-aids were useless. I was lucky. I never had any full blown blisters. Many hikers suffered with horrible blisters that became infected.

I stopped at the Laundromat in Kent, Connecticut, the Laundromat in Dalton, Massachusetts, and the Redwood Motel in Williamsport, Massachusetts. That helped me clean up and greatly improved my morale.

I preferred walking in the rain. The mosquitoes I endured, but they bothered me. The rain kept them at bay. When it wasn't raining, they made up for lost time.

There were way too many thunderstorms. I hated those thunderstorms. The forest, with its natural canopy of shade, became dark. When there was a flash of lightning, it was bright. Once I saw the lightning I would cringe, anticipating the loud crack of thunder. The Trail was muddy and the rocks and roots were slick. It took a lot of concentration to stay upright. I fell quite a few times. In areas where I had to focus on a dangerous descent I was extra cautious and never fell. On a number of occasions when I had gotten past the tricky area and was out of danger I would slip on a slick rock and fall. That was irritating!

During this two week period of heavy rain I hiked through the happy hustle and bustle of people picnicking next to Bear Mountain. I tried to catch up to Strider but ended up camped on top of a mountain under a star filled sky. The next morning I saw the most gorgeous sunrise of my hike and ate juicy blueberries without having to get out of my tent. I camped in a picture postcard setting next to Limestone Spring lean-to and drank pure, cool, water from a limestone spring. I didn't for a moment consider quitting.

Spending ten minutes in the smelly, negative, Congdon shelter was all I could take. I was glad to be tenting. I set up my tent away from the shelter and had a good night's sleep as the rain gently pattered on the fabric of my tent.

I hiked 23 miles the next day in the rain and mud. It was a chilly, windy day. At noon, I stopped at a shelter for lunch. There was a hiker in his sleeping bag. He was lethargic. I tried to get him talking without much luck. When he did speak, he wasn't making much sense. I wasn't sure if it was hypothermia, drugs, or what. I suggested he eat something for warmth and energy. He tried a power bar. It took him forever as he studied how to open the wrapper. After eating the power bar he went back to sleep. He was spooky.

I pulled into Story Spring shelter just before nightfall, set up my tent in a lovely area, and called it a day. It drizzled a little the next morning but this was the day when the constant rains finally ended. For the rest of the hike the rainfall was normal - maybe once or twice a week.

This was the first part of August and the temperatures were just about perfect in the mountains. The shade of the trees helped keep it delightful. It was hot in the towns below. When I first started my hike, I thought I was going to need suntan lotion. I even brought along two regular sized plastic tubes of it. I didn't use suntan lotion once during my hike. I discarded the first tube in Damascus, Virginia and the second in Duncannon, Pennsylvania. I never used any chap stick either.

This was a pleasant hiking day. I enjoyed soaking up the sun and didn't push the pace. I covered 15 miles. I ended the day at the William B. Douglas shelter. It was a half mile off of the Trail. A lot of that half mile was spent walking over planks to keep out of swamps and off of a fragile area completely covered with moss. The shelter was built in 1956, right when Supreme Court Justice William Douglas who was an avid hiker, was at his peak. Pun intended. The shelter was next to a pond. It was kind of marshy. It looked ideal for moose. I had seen my first moose poop earlier in the day and I was hopeful. No luck.

I was running low on food and the next morning headed three miles off- Trail to the Bromley Market to re-supply. I passed the Bromley Ski Resort on my way to the market. This place was tourist central. There was a ski lodge with a spacious, inviting, interior that included a huge plate glass window overlooking the valley below, a stone fireplace, and a long bar. There was an apparel shop with fancy, pricey, clothes, little bistros that served latte's and croissants, a Ben and Jerry's ice cream shop, a place for hamburgers and hot dogs, and a busy outside bar. There were lots of rides and kids were screaming and shouting in enjoyment. People were taking a ski lift to the top of Bromley Mountain for the beautiful views. There was a toboggan-like ride to the bottom. It looked like everyone was having a good time. It had that same positive energy I felt from the picnickers at Bear Mountain Pond.

The Bromley Market was little more than a filling station. I had a hard time finding anything suitable for backpacking. I mainly ended up with sugary junk food and spent sixty-five dollars for it. The man at the check-out counter was interested in my hike and asked:

"How many miles do you have left to the end of your hike?" I said with sincere enthusiasm. "Only five hundred miles to go!"

He looked at me like I was crazy and laughed: "You've got Five! Hundred! Miles!......That's a Looong Way!"

I guess it was a matter of perspective.

On the way back to the Trail, I couldn't resist. I stopped at a little bistro and had a mocha latte. The Trail followed a ski trail for half a mile until it reached the top of the Bromley Ski Area. That was a steep trail. It had to have been an advanced slope. I could see people on the ski lift heading to the top. It was a hot day, I was sweating profusely, and I was jealous. It was a clear day and the views were excellent. My guidebook said there was a five state view from this area.

I was glad to be heading back into the woods and away from so many people. I entered a beautiful area with healthy forest and an abundance of spruce trees. When I reached the top of Peru Peak it reminded me a lot of Maine with the moss, spruce trees, and dense forest. There was even moose poop on the ground.

Moose droppings looked like rabbit droppings on steroids. They must have good digestive systems because their droppings were uniform, circular, about an inch in diameter, and covered an area of about two feet. One of my goals was to see a moose. From here until the end of my journey I saw a lot of moose droppings. If they looked fresh I would stop, scan the area, and listen for any unusual sounds. Sometimes I would find a moose pathway and follow it off-Trail for a while but I never ran into any moose along the pathway. I was willing to try anything to see a moose - even reverse psychology. I told many people during my hike that I didn't want to see any bears and I saw eighteen. I started telling people I didn't want to see any moose.

I arrived at the Peru Peak shelter just before dark. There was a good group of Boy Scouts using the shelter. They invited me to share the shelter with them but I found a spot under tall spruce to put my tent. Peru Peak was my first fee site. The site caretaker collected my five dollars. In Vermont, some areas had so much use that The Green Mountain Club which maintained the Trail and shelters charged $5 for an overnight stay. I have never heard so much bitching and moaning from hikers. I stayed at three fee sites. They were clean, well maintained, and each had a caretaker. To me, it was money well spent.

Within a mile of the Peru Peak shelter I was walking alongside a beautiful pond. I could hear the water lapping against the shore. I looked into the clear water and could see stones and vegetation on the bottom. It was a still day and the water rippled as ducks paddled by. I listened to the cry of loons and looked up to see large birds soaring on thermals. A smell of pines was in the air. I only hiked nine miles that day but I was in no hurry. I was soaking in the beauty.

I reached the Little Rock Pond tenting area by 4:00 pm. It was within twenty yards of the pond. Children were splashing in the water and having a good time. I set up my tent in a spacious area. It was a lovely campsite. This had been an enjoyable day with blue sunny skies, no rain, and not too much climbing. The Trail had been muddy but manageable. As I set up my tent I felt relaxed, almost drowsy. The group that had been swimming in the pond came back to their campsite. There were eight kids between 10 and 12 and two counselors in their early twenties who had spiked green hair. They had an excellent rapport with their kids. They took off the next morning in a tight formation with one counselor in front and the other in back. It reminded me of a mama quail and her babies.

I lay on top of my air mattress with the intention of relaxing before going to sleep. The two previous weeks had been a struggle. I was pleasantly tired. I listened to the kids playing hide and seek. Little Panther was counting down from twenty. The next thing I knew it was midnight and I was chilly. I got into my sleeping blanket and fell into a deep sleep.

At 6:00 am, I heard the crystal clear call of a loon. I never could get enough of that melancholy, haunting, primeval sound. Two sounds make me feel a part of my ancestors - the soulful howl of a coyote and the cry of a loon. There was only one piercing call - Nature's alarm clock.

After a long, refreshing sleep, I was ready to go the next morning. The Trail followed the pond for another mile then headed up into the forest. The forest for the next four miles was covered with Christmas trees of all sizes. There were so many Christmas trees that I hummed, whistled, and sang Christmas songs: "Oh Christmas Tree. Oh Christmas Tree..." Instead of a ground cover of ferns or moss, the ground cover was tens of thousands of tiny Christmas trees. It was absolutely beautiful.

In the middle of this abundance of Christmas trees, I hiked through an area called White Rocks. There were white rocks of all shapes and sizes. I found a perfect place to take a break. It had rocks at the right height to sit on, a soft fragrant matting of pine needles, and tall pines for shade. Next to my rest spot, hikers over the years had taken small white rocks and built little rock sculptures in creative Feng Shui formations. Four more miles of hiking and I reached the top of Bear Mountain with views of the Hudson River valley and the New York City skyline.

I finished the day at the Clarendon shelter. My campsite was next to a fallen pine tree on a level area covered with pine needles. It was in a thick forest with a clear mountain stream. There was a dirt pathway that went right by my tent. It was the old Crown Point Military Road built during the French and Indian War. A ridge runner was staying at the shelter and was soon joined by a couple of thru-hikers. We were the only people at the shelter that night.

All the ridge runners that I met loved their job. This guy gave me the history of the area and showed me where the original Appalachian Trail from the late twenties passed through. That night the sound of a flute filled the air. The flute player had to have been a professional. He or she played tunes dating back a century or more. It was hauntingly beautiful.

I hiked 17 miles from Clarendon shelter to Tucker Johnson shelter. On the hike up Killington Mountain I was passed by Wiss-Pee. He stopped and introduced himself. I was delighted to finally meet him. Wiss-Pee, Strider, and Ned The Fed, were the three hikers I was trying to catch before I stopped at my sister's house in Afton, Virginia. I came so close to catching all three. I started seeing Wiss-Pee's shelter journal entries a little before the Roan Mountains in Tennessee. He didn't get sucked into the town "vortex" like other hikers. When I first saw his journals, he was five days ahead of me. If I picked up a day on him it felt like a real accomplishment. When I averaged 20.6 miles a day for eleven days before getting to my sister's home, I finally put in the mileage to catch him. I was within a day of him when I reached Rockfish Gap. He was twenty-three and had recently graduated from college. After reading his journals for so long I was expecting a person who was positive, upbeat, enthusiastic, and thoroughly enjoying his hike. That was exactly what he was. I enjoyed talking with him but it was late afternoon on a muggy day. We were both swatting mosquitoes and it was getting uncomfortable standing still. I let him continue up the Trail. He was heading to a wedding about the same time I was going to visit my brother Doug and his wife Ingrid, and we figured we would meet again. I did see him turn a corner and disappear into the woods about forty miles from Katahdin. He had just left a shelter which I was approaching. His journal entry said he had seen a huge bull moose an hour earlier. I was in the same area about that time and didn't see it. Wiss-Pee summited Katahdin on the 21st of September. That was fitting, since he always seemed to be a day or two ahead of me.

I camped uphill from the Tucker Johnson shelter. This was where the Long Trail parted with the Appalachian Trail. The shelter was dark and uninviting and there was a mud bog right in front of it. It was almost impossible not to step in the mud before entering the shelter. The shelter floor was caked with mud. I was the only person in the area until after I had gotten into bed. It rained hard that night to add muck to the Trail. The next morning as I was taking down my tent a friendly yellow lab came up from the shelter to visit. Such a nice dog. He just came by to say hi and get petted and didn't overstay his welcome. Everyone in the shelter was asleep when I walked by. The dog was sleeping beside his master. He opened his eyes, his tail went thump, thump, thump, thump, against the shelter floor, then he closed his eyes and went back to sleep.

I descended the next four miles to Kent Pond. It was a tourist destination. Many people were heading to Thundering Falls. This area fit my idea of what Vermont should look like. The forest was full of maple trees. A few were starting to change color. A winding country road wandered past white wooden houses, weathered barns, and corn fields.

I arrived at the Wintturi shelter at 6:00 pm. Vermont had beautiful camping areas at almost every shelter. This was another one. A section hiker was already at the shelter and had an excellent fire going. I was a fire appreciator and would bring in wood to feed it but I never made a fire the whole trip. Of all the campfires, this was the best. This man was the Tiger Woods of fire making. When I told him so, he beamed with pride. His fire radiated heat. He had eight big branches burning at once. Each branch was half in the fire and half out. As the wood burned down, he pushed the unburned part of the branch into the fire. The burning wood snapped and popped and sparks flew high into the air. After dark it was even more impressive. The flames danced around the fire and when Firemaster went in to tend it, his face glowed in the yellow light.

At 8:00 pm I finished my dinner and was ready to leave the shelter and find a spot to put my tent. Firemaster kept letting me know there was plenty of room in the shelter. We were the only two people there. I finally realized he was afraid of the dark. Fortunately, Pickle and Trusty came in and wanted to stay in the shelter. I had another good night's sleep. I had been hiking for 51 straight days and was a weary hiker. My mind and body were ready for rest at night and I felt lucky to be getting some refreshing sleep.

From Wintturi shelter I hiked 21 miles to Happy Hill shelter. There were a number of road crossings and it felt like the Trail was too close to neighborhoods during much of the day's hike. I knew that fifteen miles into the hike the Trail was going to go right through the small town of West Hartford, Vermont. A southbound hiker had talked earlier about having a chocolate malt at the village store. I had that running through my mind all fifteen miles - a chocolate malt. A smooth, creamy, delicious, chocolate malt. I could feel the cool, malt flavored, chocolate ice cream in my mouth as it delighted my taste buds. It would be so thick I would have to spoon it into my mouth. Spoonful after delicious spoonful. As I approached town the superlatives describing MY chocolate malt increased. I crossed into West Hartford over an old iron bridge and saw the store in the distance. I was walking as fast as my little legs would carry me. When I got there I eagerly walked up the steps and pulled on the door - and pulled again. It was closed! NNNNNNNNOOOOOOOOOOOOOOOOOOO!!!!!!

On Sunday it only stayed open until 2:00 pm. Being a mature adult and weighing all the options I had available to handle this setback, I chose to pout!

"No grocery store closes before 7:00 pm. What a hick town! What a little Podunk! Hick! Town! Closing at 2:00 pm! What is this?"

I crossed through the little PISS ANT town of West Hartford and headed back into the forest. The next four miles were spent in a dark funk! I made it to Happy Hill shelter at 7:00 pm. "What's so happy about it?" I still wasn't ready to let go of my well-deserved self-pity.

I took off early the next morning. I was eagerly looking forward to my visit with Doug, Ingrid, and their two daughters, Aurora and Karin. The Trail passed through the town of Norwich, Vermont. As I was walking through a neighborhood, a guy in his pajamas and bathrobe headed to the sidewalk to pick up his newspaper. We nodded. It reminded me of how far removed I was from everyday life. Eventually I crossed a bridge over the Connecticut River and entered Hanover.

Walking into Hanover with my backpack I didn't feel out of place at all. I have always enjoyed the youthful energy of a college town. The Trail took me to the town square. I turned right on Main Street. There was a table set up outside of Lou's Bakery with all kinds of baked goods. I picked a big sweet roll covered with chocolate frosting and a delicious cup of coffee. I took out my little clear plastic wallet that kept my money waterproof. I had change in with my bills and when I opened the wallet, some of the change dropped to the ground. I looked scruffy. I was dirty and smelly. As I was getting ready to bend down to pick up my change, a very patrician man in his late seventies in a suit and tie gave me a disdainful look and said: "You go ahead and pick it up. You probably need it." I picked up the money and put it into the tip jar. It reinforced my decision to shave my scruffy beard as soon as I reached Doug and Ingrid's and a picture was taken of it. I was always scratching that beard. I didn't like it. I was glad to be rid of it. From then on I shaved about once a week.

After I finished the roll and coffee I went back for one covered with gooey cinnamon and more coffee. I continued my hike with a sugary buzz.

I made a left on Lebanon Street and followed it to the Hanover Food Co-op. From the Co-op, I passed the Dartmouth College soccer fields, and headed back into the woods. I had nine more miles to Doug and Ingrid's. They lived less than two miles from the Appalachian Trail in Etna, New Hampshire. Doug sent me an email before I started my hike: "We'll look forward to a fit and dirty hiker showing up someday!" I remembered that. It motivated me. It was a milestone I wanted to accomplish. I really did want to show up at his house as a fit and dirty hiker - and I did!

I spent two days with Doug and his family before they headed to Maine on a vacation. It was a fun visit. After they left, I had the house to myself. In the afternoon I started reading a book by Terry Pratchett. I closed my eyes and woke up the next morning. I planned on heading back to the Trail but it felt so good just being lazy, I decided to spend another day. I had a good breakfast, lay down and snoozed. I had some lunch; then snoozed until 7:00 pm. I had some dinner. Since I had slept all day, I was worried I would be awake all night. I went to bed at 9:00 pm and slept like a log until 7:00 the next morning. My weary body was ready for some deep sleep and got it.

I had a leisurely breakfast and headed to the Trail. I hiked up Moose Mountain. I only hiked eight miles that day and stopped at Trapper John shelter. I was sore and it took another day to work back into the hike. There were a lot of people at the shelter that night. A trail angel had brought Big Macs, fries, cokes, and beer, and everyone was gathered around the fire, chatting and enjoying the food. The trail angel brought along his nine year old daughter and she was talking with Nature. I hadn't seen Nature since early Pennsylvania. There were a lot of people around and I nodded to her and she looked right through me. Huh? If she didn't want to talk to me, no problem. I wasn't going to push it. There were a lot of tents set up that night. It was hard finding a good area to put my tent. I slept on a slope, squeezed in between two big rocks.

The next morning, people were waiting in line to use the privy. I never could understand why people would use those nasty, smelly, privys when they had the great outdoors. I headed out at 8:00 am. After a three mile descent from Trapper John shelter, I passed Dorchester Road. There was a swampy pond on my right. The pathway was almost hidden in the thick grass and there were mosquitoes everywhere. A handwritten sign was stuck in the ground next to the Trail. "Free Ice Cream - Follow the path across the road to the blue house." How could I turn that down? I headed over. The man giving away the free ice cream stopped his conversation with another hiker and made me feel welcome. After I finished the Eskimo Pie, I plunged my hand into a tub full of ice and grabbed a coke. I paid fifty cents for it. The man had been doing this for years. He had a register where he had us put our trail name, where we were from, when we started our hike, and our age. He was in his seventies and just a generous, outgoing, social, person. He genuinely enjoyed talking with us. Looking at the register, I could see all the people ahead of me who had stopped for ice cream and their ages. Interesting.

Refreshed, I headed back to the Trail and started a long, rugged climb to the top of Smarts Mountain. It went from 850' to 3,230' in a little over four miles. Nature and her hiking partner caught up to me. A big smile was on her face: "Wingo? Is that you? You shaved your beard. I saw your name on the register. It's me. Nature."

We hiked off and on together through the tough presidential range of New Hampshire for the next 95 miles. I enjoyed her company. Bronco and Nature invited me to hike with them. Bronco had thru-hiked the Appalachian Trail the year before but because of illness or injury was not able to hike a forty mile section which he was now completing. He was a super-enthusiastic hiker. He lived for hiking. He knew the history of the Trail and practically every person that hiked it for the past two years. He was a non-stop talker but I didn't get tired of listening. His enthusiasm was infectious. He set the pace when the three of us hiked together and he was good at it. We covered a lot of ground and broke a good sweat but he stayed within our ability.

I hadn't seen Nature since Pennsylvania and was trying to get caught up. As we were hiking, I asked Nature a question and Bronco in his enthusiasm, answered it. He did it a second time. On the third time, Nature and I burst out laughing. Bronco looked back sheepishly: "You were asking Nature that question, weren't you?" We all laughed.

We took a break on a rock slab on a ridge. The views were awesome. We saw a fire tower on a mountaintop way in the distance. Bronco looked at his map and said it was the fire tower on top of Smarts Mountain. It was going to be a long, uphill climb to get to it. Surprisingly, it took only a couple of hours. Bronco set a good pace. We all climbed to the top of the tower, built in the 1920's, and enjoyed the view.

We were trying to get to Hexacuba shelter six miles away but were running out of daylight. We found a beautiful area next to a rapidly flowing stream to camp. I put my tent in a great spot close enough to the water where the sound blocked out any other noise. There was a pool of calm water away from the main current and a flat slab of rock came to its edge. It was perfect for dunking, tired, swollen feet into the ice cold mountain water.

For dinner, I tried a Mountain House Lasagna and a Mountain House Scrambled Eggs and Ham. This was the first time I had tried freeze dried food on my hike. It was pretty good. I hadn't eaten freeze dried food in over twenty years and back then it wasn't very good. I enjoyed chatting with such upbeat, enthusiastic people. I could tell there was nowhere in the world they would rather be than right where they were - and they knew it.

The next morning when I got ready to take down my tent I noticed a dark yellow stain at the foot of the tent. Since the sound of the stream had blocked any other sound in the night, some animal had peed on my tent and I didn't hear it. That mark is still on my tent. I could have easily wiped it off. I don't know why, but I never did.

The morning started with an immediate climb of 1,400' to the top of Mount Cube. The forest in this area was full and healthy. Spruce and pines were the predominant trees. After a difficult 17 mile day where I worked for every mile, I finished at Jeffers Brook shelter. By 8:00 pm I was so tired I fell into a deep sleep. Nature, who was tented nearby, thought she heard a moose in the night.

We were about to enter the White Mountains. I will try to give you an idea what the Trail was like in the Whites. It was very difficult. There were a number of days when I only averaged one mile per hour. At the bottom of the mountain the trees were tall and closely spaced. There was a lot of vegetation; mainly ferns and moss. There were small streams. Since it had rained heavily in the previous weeks there were many mud puddles. The Trail was covered with slippery roots and rocks. The roots spread out horizontally from the trees. They were of different sizes and shapes and were super slick when wet. The rocks along the Trail were of many sizes and shapes and tightly packed together. Much of the time I was hiking on nothing but rocks. In areas where the pathway was dirt and rocks, it was more rocks than dirt. It never allowed me to stride out. As I was climbing up the mountain, there would be long slabs of rock. They could be 100 feet wide and go up 100 yards or more. At times they were fairly steep and I would be climbing on all fours. These rock surfaces were very slick when wet. Sometimes I had to tack like a sailboat following a zig zag pattern to find the safest route up the steep rock. From halfway up the mountain on, there were many rock slabs along the pathway where the climbs were very steep - some almost vertical. They ranged in height from 10 feet to 30 feet or more. I had to find handholds and footholds in the natural formation of the rock. I would look for bumps, uneven areas, cracks and crevices. There were times when I would get halfway up a rock slab and couldn't go any farther. I would head back down and look for another route. Sometimes at the side of the rock slab there were tree roots and small trees that I could grab onto. I had to be cautious because many times they were loose and could give way. This was a dirty, often muddy alternative, and at the end of the day, my hands, arms, and legs were caked with dirt.

My biggest fear was that I would be 30 feet up a vertical climb and have my pack weight tip me backwards. I knew if that happened there would be no Plan B. It almost happened once. I started to sway backwards, caught it, and was super cautious from then on.

As the Trail got closer to the tree line, the trees became smaller and more tightly spaced. There were bogs in this area and I would frequently be walking over wooden planks - often wobbly, rotten, wooden planks.

Above tree line the Trail, if anything, got rockier. There were rocks of all sizes that were jumbled together. The vegetation in this area was small and clung tightly to the ground. There were even tiny blueberry bushes with tiny tart blueberries.

Heading down the mountain I would extend my hiking poles to their full length. I felt like a long legged spider, placing the poles down the pathway and making sure they were firmly planted before moving forward. There were times I would look over the edge of a 20' vertical slab of rock and not see a way down. These areas had my undivided attention. If I made a mistake and fell I knew I would be badly hurt.

Once I adjusted my thinking, I enjoyed these areas. They were like good puzzles. There had to be a way down and I had to use my imagination and physical skills to solve the puzzle. I used many techniques to get down. Sometimes the hiking poles would work. I would stretch the fully extended poles down to a crevice or small flat area on the rock and slowly work my way down. Many times I would toss my stout hiking poles to a lower level and find handholds and footholds to work my way down the rock slab. Sometimes I would angle down to the edge of the slab and use small trees and roots the rest of the way down. When I reached the bottom of a rock slab the pathway would continue to be steep and rocky. I used my hiking poles to spider my way down these areas.

At times there were rocks the size of cars that were jumbled next to one another. I had to use my imagination on these descents, too. I used a combination of hiking poles, hand and footholds, sliding down on my butt, and extending my legs over a rock as far as they would go and dropping the rest of the way.

As I neared the bottom of the mountain there were fewer vertical drops and rock slabs. The trees became taller, streams started to show up again, and the steepness of the Trail diminished. I always hiked downhill alone and at my own slow pace. Frequently, I would say to myself that this was supposed to be a hiking path, not an obstacle course! I said that frequently throughout New Hampshire and Maine!

Bronco, Nature, and I headed out from Jeffers Brook shelter at 8:00 in the morning. As we started our first climb, there was a crutch hanging from a tree. Next to the crutch was a handwritten sign: "Welcome to the Whites! Everything else was just a warm-up for what you are about to experience. Good Luck!"

I had been waiting for this the whole trip. Everyone talked about the Whites with awe and respect. When I first started my hike I looked forward to the challenge of the Whites with arrogance. Having hiked many higher mountains in New Mexico with long climbs and descents, I thought the Whites would be more of the same, only easier. The mountains in New Mexico were higher and the paths were steep, but far less rocky. Once the Trail became rocky from Pennsylvania on, I began to realize what a challenge this was going to be.

I know I trash talked the Whites with both Johanna and Bob, and Doug and Ingrid. Something about "Kicking the White's butt!" I could tell they weren't buying it, and sadly, I realized my false bravado for what it was. By the time I reached the Whites, my arrogance was gone. My conditioning was good, but my body had hiked 1,800 miles. I was physically tired. I knew I could coast the rest of the hike and make it to Katahdin in plenty of time so I focused on a steady pace.

The Whites zapped me physically. They progressively got harder and I could feel my strength waning. I averaged less than 10 miles a day in the Whites, but that included two days that I didn't hike. If I hiked 10 miles a day in some areas, I was proud of it and not losing ground to other hikers. This was extremely difficult hiking. There was one period after Mt. Washington where I had days of 7.1, 7.8, and 5.9 miles and that was all I could do. I was physically and mentally drained at the end of those days. I ran the gamut of emotions on my hike through the Whites. It was extremely challenging but I wouldn't trade those memories for anything!

When Bronco, Nature, and I left Jeffers Brook shelter our elevation was 1,350'. By the time we reached the top of Mt. Moosilauke, four and a half miles later, we were at 4,802'. We were above tree line and it was a windy, clear day with excellent 360 degree views. People had hiked in this area for many years. At the top, there were big rocks next to the Trail where they had chiseled their names and the date. A few were from 1880 and before. Seeking shelter from the chilly wind, I sat on the ground next to the remnants of a wall of the Prospect House built in 1860. It was a popular tourist spot that burned down in 1942.

Some parts of the Trail in the Whites dated back to the 1850's and had been so heavily used over the years, the tread from boots had smoothed the tops of rocks along the pathway and left them with a darker color. Hiking over a wide rocky area of the Trail, I could see the most popular option hikers had chosen over the years.

I was the first to arrive at the top of Mt Moosilauke. Pretty soon, Nature and Bronco showed up with Juice and Mama Llama. Juice and Mama Llama were a retired couple who I first met outside of Joe's Coffee in Branchville, New Jersey. Everyone set their camera timers and we took group pictures. The pictures show the mood we were in - glad to be on top after such a long, hard, climb.

Bronco had hiked this area in the past and warned us the descent off of Mt. Moosilauke was going to be very difficult. Having hiked with him, I trusted his judgment. He was right. It was the most difficult descent of my trip. The pathway down followed a swift stream with many beautiful waterfalls. With the humidity and churned up water from the waterfalls, the pathway was wet and slippery. There were areas of nearly vertical descents on slippery rock slabs with scary drops. Many times I tossed my hiking poles down to a lower level and used my hands to maneuver.

Some areas had long rock walls that were so sheer that rebar or wooden blocks were added. I much preferred the rebar. I could grab on to the bar and slowly work my way down, always having a foot and hand in contact with the rebar at the same time. I didn't like the wooden blocks at all! They were only put on areas with long, steep, descents, and usually had moisture on them which made them slippery. I didn't trust them. I would put my hiking poles on the block below and make sure the poles were stable. I had to lean forward when I placed my hiking poles on the block and I could feel the weight of my backpack pushing me forward. I would then step down to the block trying to keep my boot from sliding off the wet, slippery, block. I could sometimes feel the boot wanting to slip. It was very uncomfortable.

It was a long, difficult descent and I was glad when I made it to the bottom. It was exhilarating, though. When I reached the bottom I met a young woman going in the opposite direction. She was eyeing the steep rock climb ahead. She looked nervous. I didn't try to re-assure her. I told her: "Take your time and be very careful!" There was an Appalachian Trail sign at the bottom that said: "This trail is extremely tough. If you lack experience please use another trail. Take special care at the Cascades to avoid tragic results."

There was another long, steep climb to the top of Mt. Wolf. Three quarters of the way up, I caught up with Juice and Mama Llama who were filtering water. It was 7:00 pm. My first day in the Whites had been very strenuous. I was tired. I knew I had to hike fast for the next hour to get to the Eliza Brook campsite before dark. When I talked with Juice and Mama Llama, I told them that if this was all the Whites had to offer; then they wouldn't be a problem. Mr. Macho. I don't know why I said something that stupid. Mama Llama, who was a realist, said that the day's hike had completely tired her out. I wanted to agree with her but I couldn't back out.

Hiking as fast as I could and making pretty good time in the rocky conditions, I managed to make it to the campsite before dark. It was dark by the time I had my tent up. Juice and Mama Llama walked by my tent in the dark and set up camp. We were the only ones at the camping area that night. It was a beautiful area next to a slowly flowing stream with brownish water and a swiftly flowing stream with clear clean looking water. Guess which was the recommended water source and the source I didn't use? I heard a lot of noise in the night but was too tired to get out of my tent to see if it was a moose. It could have been, though. There were fresh droppings in the area.

Juice and Mama Llama were early risers and were long gone by the time I got out of my sleeping bag at 7:00 am. I was greeted with a 2,000' climb to the top of South Kinsman Mountain; then a slight descent to North Kinsman. I spent most of the day hiking alone. It was difficult rocky hiking. I worked hard to get in 11 miles.

I was getting low on food. The last time I re-supplied was at my brothers. I had gotten a lot of freeze dried Mountain House dinners. They saved on weight and tasted pretty good but I underestimated how many I would need for five days of hiking. A Mountain House dinner was two servings and didn't nearly fill me up. I wasn't full after two Mountain House dinners and ate a lot of my trail mix to compensate. I should have re-supplied when I reached Franconia Notch but didn't want to hitch eight miles into North Woodstock, New Hampshire, re-supply, and hitch eight miles back. I thought I had enough to last until I made it to Crawford Notch, twenty- five miles up the Trail. I was thinking in normal miles - not miles in the Whites. That was my mistake. My appetite was ravenous and my food supply dwindled much faster than I anticipated.

From Franconia Notch to my day's destination, Liberty Springs tent site, the Trail was steep but relatively smooth. It was a hot day but I still had some energy so I tried to see if I could hike the 2.6 miles in an hour. I gave it my best shot. Salty sweat was stinging my eyes and dripping off of my nose. My shirt was soaked. I didn't come close. It took me an hour and a half.

Liberty Springs tent site was a pay tent site. There were fifteen platforms. A few were big enough for up to four tents on a platform. Most were just big enough for one tent. The caretaker came by and took my $8.00. The campsite was in a lovely location. I saw an excellent sunset as I was cooking the last of my Mountain House dinners. The next morning I finished my last four Pop Tarts for breakfast. The day looked to be a big one. Liberty Springs tent site was on Little Haystack Mountain and I had a 1,000' climb to the top. During the day I would be climbing Mt. Lincoln, Mt. Lafayette, Mt. Garfield, and heading up South Twin Mountain before stopping at Galehead hut.

This was a fun day of hiking. A lot of the Trail was above tree line and extremely rocky and challenging. Much of the groundcover was tight to the ground. I could only imagine the cold winds, ice, and snow that the plants and grasses endured in the harsh winter. There were berry bushes with brightly colored, delicate little flowers. Areas were covered with short, brown grasses flowing smoothly in the breeze. Signs encouraged hikers to stay on the pathway to protect the fragile vegetation.

Many climbs and descents were over rocks where there wasn't a defined pathway. I hiked from cairn to cairn in these areas. Cairns were rocks stacked together that could be three feet to over ten feet high and were placed every 100 feet or so along the pathway above tree line. In areas where the pathway wasn't well defined the cairns would be every 50 feet.

The weather was constantly changing. Climbing up Mt. Lincoln it was sunny and breezy. I could see clouds forming in the distance. I could see forever. There were small towns and shiny lakes in the distance. I could see tall mountains that were tiny blurs on the horizon. I knew eventually I would be climbing them. That was the first and about the only time the enormity of my 2,178 mile thru-hike sank in. I saw those blurs on the horizon and realized how much effort it would take to get to them and what a small percentage that distance was of the whole hike.

From Mt. Lincoln, I started to climb Mt. Lafayette. The clouds rolled in, it became cooler, and I put on my yellow windbreaker. By the time I reached the top of Mt. Lafayette, it was foggy, windy, and cold. I added my fleece pullover and hunkered down next to the three foot wall of a long abandoned building trying to stay warm and out of the cold wind. I was finding it hard to ration my food. I was down to a hand full of trail mix and a couple of Snickers bars. I ate a Snickers bar. I was hoping to wait out the fog but it didn't look like it was going away anytime soon so I headed out. I was grateful for the cairns. Eventually the clouds moved through and I was back in the warm sun. The views were unlimited. It truly was as far as the eyes could see. I remember thinking: "This is why I'm hiking the Appalachian Trail!"

From Mt. Lafayette I began a descent to Garfield Pond. It was a big pond surrounded by tall trees. It was a tranquil setting and I took a break and enjoyed it. I finished the last of my food. Climbing up Mt. Garfield was steep and difficult. I was burning a lot of energy and out of food. I made a serious mistake not re-supplying at Franconia Notch. I could no longer afford to make dumb mistakes. Unlike when I had almost run out of food hiking through the Smokies, now I didn't have any fat reserves. If I touched my sides and lower back where I carry my fat reserves those areas were as solid as my arm muscles. I knew I was close to feeding on my muscle. I still had four more miles of extremely hard hiking. I was averaging one mile per hour in this area.

I did something that you can't imagine how hard it was for me to do. A hiker passed me on the climb. I asked him if he had some power bars that I could buy. I explained my situation. He looked at me suspiciously at first; then his generosity came through. He gave me three power bars and a package of trail mix and wouldn't take any money for it. I was embarrassed and grateful. I ate the power bars on the spot and held onto the trail mix. I caught up to him while he was taking a break and he gave me an apple and some grapes. He was a school teacher and a good man. He empathized with my situation. He told me he had been living in Colorado in the 70's and was down to a ketchup sandwich when he had gotten a job in the knick of time. Those four miles to Galehead hut were extremely difficult and I was grateful to have some food in my belly. I chastised myself for my lack of judgment. Lack of food could have left me light headed in those high mountains. I made it to Galehead hut at 5:00 pm.

There were seven huts in the White Mountains. I stayed at Galehead hut, Lakes of the Clouds hut, Madison Spring hut, and Carter Notch hut. They bring back fond memories. All four were built around 1915. They were all extensively remodeled and were in beautiful locations. They were solid structures that were well insulated with thick windows built to withstand the harsh elements. The highest wind speed ever recorded - 231 mph - was recorded in the Whites. They varied in size from thirty people to the most popular hut - Lakes of the Clouds - with space for 95 people. The only way to get to the huts was by hiking, although most huts had trails of different skill levels that led to them. They were very popular and a great way to have a vacation. There were lots of families hiking from hut to hut. People spent $85 to stay at a hut. The huts were close enough together so that even the slowest hiker could hike from one hut to the next, although some hikers made it to the hut after dark, totally exhausted. Hikers could spend a week or more hiking from hut to hut. For their $85 they got a bunk and a blanket. Sometimes there were separate areas for men and women. Other times it was a big room that had bunks next to the wall, all the way around the room and a row of bunks down the center. Sometimes the bunks were stacked four high. It jammed a lot of people into a small area but the hikers wanted this experience. The $85 paid for breakfast which was hearty and included bacon, ham, eggs, pancakes, oatmeal, baked cinnamon coffee cake, and plenty of coffee. Lunch was soup and baked bread. Dinner, I considered gourmet, but I was starving at the time. There was a spacious dining area with benches where everyone gathered throughout the day when they were not hiking. They made new friends, chatted, read, and played games. These were outdoor people who were here to have a good time. It was a jovial atmosphere. The staff was called the croo. They were college students and graduate students who had a great summer job and knew it. The competition to get one of those jobs must have been fierce and the croo members I met were top notch. Whoever did the hiring was looking for something specific in the applicants and found it. Thru-hikers had the opportunity to spend the night at a hut and out of the sometimes harsh elements. It was called "work for stay". When a thru-hiker reached a hut he could ask the croo leader for work for stay. The Thru-Hikers' Companion Guidebook said that most huts would only grant a couple of hikers work for stay each night. If a hiker was fortunate enough to be given work for stay he slept in the dining room after the guests went to bed. The work was whatever needed doing - washing the dishes, organizing the pantry, de-icing the freezer, sweeping the floor. If he wasn't assigned a chore that night, he would be assigned a job the next morning. It was easy work. I don't think I ever spent more than 20 minutes working. There was a rule that didn't set well with a lot of thru-hikers. While the regular customers were having breakfast and dinner the thru- hikers had to wait outside. This was the rule and thru-hikers knew it before asking for work for stay. I had no problem with it. After dinner, work for stay thru-hikers finished the leftovers. That was absolutely wonderful and I took full advantage of it. I didn't have to feel guilty making a pig of myself. The croo appreciated having us eat as much as we could, otherwise they would have to compost any remaining food. Whenever I asked for work for stay, I looked the croo leader in the eye. I could see the compassion in their eyes each time they said yes. The croo leaders and most of the croo were genuinely nice kids that I'm sure made their parents proud. There was a kindness about them but a toughness, too. There were some thru-hikers with chips on their shoulders who were assholes. They were quickly and firmly told to find another place to stay.

Juice and Mama Llama were already at Galehead hut when I arrived. They told me to talk to Mary, the croo leader, to ask for work for stay. I think she saw how tired I was and there was a softness in her eyes when she said yes. I was delighted. I was starving, though. I asked if there was some soup I could buy. She said there wasn't but she pointed to five brownies in a plastic container on the counter that were for sale. She said they had been there long enough and I could have them. She added some sluices of baked bread. I took my plastic container and sat down at one of the dining room tables with Juice and Mama Llama. They were busy writing home to their children so I didn't bother them. I was seated about ten feet from them. The aroma of the bread and the brownies was wonderful. There were a few flies around so I leaned over and wrapped my arms around the plastic container as I picked up pieces of bread and ate them. I know I looked like Fagan in "Oliver", greedily glancing right and left as he guarded his precious treasures. Juice inhaled deeply and said: "Wingo, that bread sure smells good." I looked at him like a dog protecting a meaty bone. Juice and Mama Llama laughed. I saw them many times for the rest of my thru-hike and took a lot of good natured ribbing. I'm afraid that will be their memory of Wingo.

A group of middle aged men came into the hut after finishing their day's hike. There was a camaraderie as they joked and talked about their hike. By 7:00 pm all the hikers made it to the hut and dinner was served. Juice, Mama Llama, and I stood outside and talked. Galehead hut was on a ridge. We watched a lovely sunset. On top of the hut was a wind turbine about the size of a weathervane that swiveled into the wind and supplied electricity for the hut. It had a propeller that was three feet in length. If the wind picked up, the speed of the propeller increased and the sound and pitch increased. It reminded me of a dentist's drill. Wind gusts would make the pitch very high.

After the regular customers finished their dinner we were invited in to finish the leftovers. There was a loaf of freshly baked bread, green beans, mashed potatoes and gravy, soup, Salisbury steak, and peach pie. I heaped my plate as full as I could get it. Mama Llama and Juice did the same. We went back for seconds and filled our plates to the brim again. As we were finishing, Mary came to the table with the remainder of the Salisbury steak. "Can anybody finish this?" I wanted to ask: "Is the Pope, Catholic?", but settled for: "You bet!" It was plain, everyday food, but it was one of the best meals of my life!

It was a cold, windy night and before falling asleep, I enjoyed listening to the wind propelling the turbine. When the pitch was especially high, it made me glad to be in my warm sleeping bag in the well-insulated hut.

The next morning, Juice and Mama Llama left early. After the guests left, I swept the dining room floor and then feasted on leftover pancakes, oatmeal and coffee cake. The croo didn't have to compost that morning. There were Snickers Bars and Power Bars for sale at the hut. I purchased six before I left. It was 15 miles to Crawford Notch but with the filling breakfast I knew I could make it.

After leaving Galehead hut there was an immediate climb from 3,800' to the top of South Twin Mountain at 4,902' and then some ridge walking to Mt. Guyot at 4,508'. It was a warm sunny morning. I passed a lot of vacationers hiking from hut to hut. They were getting their money's worth this fine day. The area captured the beauty of the Whites.

In the early afternoon, as I was high in the mountains and starting to head down to Zealand Falls hut, a fast moving thunderstorm came through. The woods, which had been light and sunny, grew dark. I could tell this was going to be a bad one. I was still high on the mountain but at least I was heading down and in fairly thick tree cover. The storm was right over me in no time. The thunder was crackling and then there was a very bright and loud: FLASH/BOOM! It was so close and startling that I jumped! I could feel the ground vibrate. That was the closest lightning strike in my entire life. It had to have been behind me because I didn't see it hit the ground. I had an incredible adrenaline surge! I took a moment to gather my wits and sat down on the Trail. That was the first and only time I didn't keep walking in a thunderstorm. As I was sitting there, I worried that a tree branch would break off in the heavy wind and fall on me. I worried about the metal hiking poles becoming lightning rods and collapsed them as small as they would go and put them under my pack. I worried about the next lightning strike because there was a lot of lightning and it was hitting close. It was a fast moving storm and only lasted about ten minutes but it felt like an eternity!

After the storm passed the Trail became muddy and slippery. Just before reaching Zealand Falls hut I slipped on some rocks and bloodied my right hand as I broke my fall. It opened a flap of skin under my right knee, too. The wounds were bloody and muddy. The hut was near so I decided to hike to the hut and clean them there. At the hut I sat on the bench on the front porch cleaning my bloody wounds and unintentionally grossed out a lot of vacationers who walked by.

I purchased some freshly baked chocolate chip cookies before heading out. There were a lot of people at the hut. It was close to Crawford Notch and there were some easy trails to get to it. A pond was in front of the hut and people were noisily playing in the water. The place felt more like a tourist attraction so I gladly put it in my rear view mirror. As I was leaving, I passed a noisy, chubby, father and his noisy, chubby 10 and 11 year old sons. They were day hiking from the hut and not carrying packs. I couldn't put them away. In fact, the kids were gaining on me. The father was yelling at the kids to slow down and wait for him. The kids weren't listening. I was distracted and when I got to a Trail junction I quickly glanced at the Trail sign, saw Crawford Notch at the bottom which I knew was my destination, and took the pathway to the left. The kids and father turned right. Great!

I passed a swampy pond that looked ideal for moose. It was slightly drizzling and raindrops were making thousands of little ripples on the water. The Trail didn't look quite as heavily used in this area. Something wasn't quite right. I looked for the white blazes of the Appalachian Trail. There weren't any. There were yellow blazes. The Thru-Hikers' Companion Guidebook said that in the White Mountains the snowfall was so deep that sometimes yellow blazes were used instead of white because white blazes could blend in with the white snow.

This would have been the perfect time to get out my Appalachian Trail map and sort this out. I didn't have an Appalachian Trail map. Maps were depressing. People who were avid map readers were depressing. I didn't want to know ahead of time how many climbs and descents I had that day or how steep they were. I wanted the Trail to surprise me. It was a pure delight to turn a corner and have a serene pond with sandy beaches appear before my eyes. I didn't want to know that in one half mile I would be approaching Moose Pond - elevation 2,417'. People who were avid map readers often psyched themselves out. If they saw on the map profile there were steep mountains the next day, they would practically go into a depression.

It was annoying when someone would take out their map during a break. I would be pleasantly rooting through my trail mix finding M&M's to pop into my mouth and would glance over and see the map reader getting agitated.

"Great! Here it comes!" I would say to myself.

"Oh no! Look at this! We've (I was always thoughtfully included.) got a monster of a climb coming up! Damn! We're going to be sweatin' like pigs on this one! Shit!"

My theory was that the Appalachian Trail was so heavily used the Trail would be well defined. My theory would have worked if it hadn't been for New Hampshire. In the Whites, the Appalachian Trail was commonly referred on signs by the name of the local trail it followed - such as the "Franconia Ridge Trail". The Franconia Ridge Trail would change to another local trail and then another and after a while it was confusing. In many areas the white blazes, just when you really needed them, were few and far between. It felt almost like an "attitude". "Hey. You've gotten this far. Figure it out!"

Believing the Thru-Hikers' Companion Guidebook, I continued on my hike for the next 8 miles until I arrived at Crawford Notch at 6:00 pm. I badly needed to re-supply and two miles to the east on U.S. 302 there was a campground and camp store where I could spend the night and re-supply. I started walking in that direction. Within five minutes a car stopped for me. The man who gave me a ride was a section hiker and was still buzzing with excitement. He had been hiking in the same area I had been hiking during the thunderstorm, only he had been above tree line. He said that lightning had been hitting close by and then he felt a buzz of electricity around him. He started running as fast as he could to get down into the trees. He said he had never been more scared in his life and was thanking God he was still alive. I can't imagine how he didn't break a leg, running with his heavy backpack on those wet, slippery, rocks, but I believed him when he said he was running. He needed to be telling this to someone and I was glad to be there for him. I told him I was hiking the Appalachian Trail and he told me I wasn't on the Appalachian Trail and was actually three miles from the campground instead of two miles. Terrific!

He drove me to the campground and went inside with me. He priced the groceries at the camp store and pointed out that they were outrageous. They were. He then drove me to a grocery store in a town four miles away, waited while I re-supplied, and took me back to the campground. From the time he picked me up on U.S. 302, to the time he dropped me off at the campground, it was cold and continuously raining. What a trail angel!

The campground was big and touristy. It had over a hundred sites for tents or trailers. It even had little cottages. I was interested in the bunkhouse for thru-hikers. I went to the office to check in. I left my backpack outside in the rain. I no longer had my beard and had shaved a day earlier at Galehead hut. I got in line in back of three people waiting to get a camping space. The lady asked everyone in front of me if they wanted a cottage or camping space. When she got to me she said: "The bunkhouse is $23." After shaving my beard, I thought people wouldn't think I was a thru-hiker. I didn't fool anyone.

I lucked out and had the bunkhouse to myself. The bed was comfortable. I locked the door and slept soundly. Nature spent the next night at the bunkhouse and said it was so full people were sleeping on the floor.

Since I hadn't hiked the actual Appalachian Trail, I knew I would have to go back to Zealand Falls hut and hike back on the Appalachian Trail. When I approached the trailhead leading back to Zealand Falls hut I passed Rock Dancer who was parked next to the trailhead and providing trail magic. He had a real variety of food - fruits, cheeses, fixings for sandwiches. A couple who had thru-hiked the AT years earlier and were living in Florida, gave Rock Dancer $200 and asked him to provide trail magic until the money ran out. I had just had my four Pop Tarts for breakfast, but at his insistence (like he was twisting my arm) I put in at least another 2,000 calories. We sat and talked as I was eating. I told him of my mistake and that I had to hike back to Zealand Falls hut and then back to where we were standing - a 15.4 mile round trip. Grrr. I was a purist and knew if I didn't go back and follow the right path it would bug me for the rest of my hike. He listened and said: "Wingo, I think I can make this easier for you." I was listening. "When the next thru-hikers come by, we will see if they will stay and hand out the food, and I will take you to a trail that is easier and closer to the hut." Fortunately, the next hikers to show up were Nature and Bronco and they were more than happy to oblige. This was Bronco's last day on the Trail. Before Rock Dancer drove me to the trailhead, I talked with Nature and agreed to meet her at 8:00 the next morning, where we were standing.

Rock Dancer drove me at least six miles to the trail. Along the way we had a good conversation. He had thru-hiked the Appalachian Trail in the late 80's. He was the most knowledgeable person I met on my hike. When we reached the trailhead, he handed me an apple and a banana and sent me on my way. Thank you, Rock Dancer.

This trail to Zealand Falls hut was like a smooth, wide boulevard. It was incredibly easy. I passed a member of the Zealand Falls hut croo who had a huge framed pack on her back and was carrying food supplies up to the hut. That was the way all huts were supplied with food. Hiking this easy trail, my attitude changed and I enjoyed the smooth, almost rock less hike through maples, oak, and pine trees. I eventually made it back to the sign where I made the wrong turn. The sign to the Ethan Pond shelter along the Appalachian Trail was as clear as day. Grrr, again.

At one point, the five mile hike from Zealand Falls hut to Ethan Pond campsite followed an old abandoned railroad bed along the side of a mountain. I passed through a lot of scree. There was a long, gradual drop to the river. I could hear the Caw Caw Caw of crows circling far below. The sounds echoed in the mountains. It was a perfect place for a lunch. Before leaving I had to try it. I yelled and heard my echo.

To get across a corner of Ethan Pond to enter the campsite, I had to rock hop across the water. There were a limited number of rocks and some goofy people had decided to stand on those rocks and have a conversation. Everyone, except the man who was lecturing, was making an effort to get out of the way. The lecturer was deliberately ignoring me. I had to step on the rock he was on so I kept moving toward it. I could see the anxiety of the people around me who were anticipating the events that were about to unfold. I stepped on the rock the man was standing on and brushed him with my backpack. He was startled. Stunned would be a better word. I could see the smiles on a couple of faces as I continued on.

This was a great place for a campsite. The caretaker who took my $8 told me there were moose in the area and often in the early morning they would be in the pond. I knew I would be getting up early so I was hoping to see one as I headed out the next morning. No luck. The Trail heading down to Crawford Notch was ideal for moose. There were fresh droppings all over the place. This was an area with lots of moss on the ground, small streams, and spruce trees that were tightly spaced. I was feeling lucky. Every time I heard a twig snap I would stand completely still and listen. No luck. I heard later that Knickers who had been close behind me had seen a big bull moose. No justice!

Bronco, in his Ford Bronco, brought Nature, Featherfoot, and Grits from the bunkhouse to the trailhead. I met them at 8:00 am. Our destination was Lakes of the Clouds hut at the base of Mt. Washington. Bronco summited Katahdin on a cloudy, rainy, day the year before and felt short changed. He was heading back to climb Katahdin on a clear, sunny, day. Grits took off while we were saying goodbye. Nature, Featherfoot, and I started out together. It was a long steep climb. I was leading and setting a good pace. We caught up to Slagline and we all took a break next to a stream and visited.

I only hiked with Featherfoot for four days but I enjoyed his company. He had recently retired. He had let his already long hair grow out for five months and it shot out at all angles. He was the poster boy for "bad hair" day. He had a long mustache that drooped over the side of his face. He had a great, spontaneous sense of humor. He could zing you but it was never hurtful. I found myself laughing whenever I was around him and I noticed everyone else was too.

Nature and I soon pulled ahead of Featherfoot and Slagline. I was still setting a good pace. It was steep, rocky climbing. On the downhill, I let Nature go ahead. That lady was in terrific shape. Since she had started her thru-hike she had lost forty pounds and was in peak condition to tackle the

Whites. I caught Grits on Webster Cliffs. I saw him for the first time when I ducked into the first shelter in Vermont to get out of the rain. He had recently retired. He lived in Georgia and had a heavy Southern accent. He had also lost forty pounds on his hike and was fit. We traveled the Trail at about the same speed and I hiked with him quite a few times all the way to the 100 mile Wilderness in Maine. He had two daughters that he stayed in touch with by phone while hiking, numerous grandchildren, and even a great grandchild. He summited Katahdin on the 25th of September.

This day of hiking drained me. The elevation was 1,277' at the trailhead when we started in the morning. We climbed to Webster Cliffs (3,350'), then Mt. Webster (3,910'). We descended and began another climb to Mt. Jackson (4,052'). We descended again to Mizpa Spring hut (3,800') and took a break. It was chilly at that altitude. I caught up to Nature at the hut and eventually Featherfoot caught up to us. There was carrot soup for sale and it was warm and good. I would gladly have called it a day but I couldn't lose face so I continued on. We all left together but separated early. Featherfoot, who would leave the Trail within seven days to compete in his 23rd straight Make A Wish Foundation Marathon got his second wind and that was the last I saw of him until I reached Lakes of the Clouds hut. He was back on the Trail three days after completing the Marathon and summited Katahdin on the 30th of September. From Mizpah hut, I climbed to Mt. Pierce (4,312'), then down again and back up to the top of Mt. Franklin (5,004'). I traveled above tree line another mile to Lakes of the Clouds hut which was in a barren rocky area at 5,012'.

When I entered Lakes of the Clouds hut at 5:00 pm I was greeted by Juice, Mama Llama, Nature, and Featherfoot. Slagline and Grits arrived within the hour. Juice told me the person to ask for work for stay was Stephanie. I didn't think my chances were very good but I asked anyway. I was delighted and grateful when she said yes. Work for stay was extended to all the thru-hikers this night although they didn't have to do that. This was an exceptionally nice croo.

There was a long bench just inside the door and we were able to stay inside while the guests had their dinner. As hikers entered the building we felt the cold outside air. This was the biggest hut of all and filled to capacity - 95 guests. The dining area was spacious and surrounded by large double paned windows. With that many people chatting while having dinner, it was noisy. I was sitting at the table with the other thru-hikers. It had been a hard day of hiking and I was tired. The warmth of the room and the constant drone of 95 people having dinner was making me drowsy. I was fighting the urge to nod off.

We had a conversation going and one of the questions was whether we were ready for the hike to end. We all answered it. We all knew there wasn't the slightest possibility any of us would quit. But were we ready for the hike to end? All of the hikers at the table had been on the Trail a month longer than I had. They were tired and the Whites were beating them up. Every one of them was over fifty and every one of them was in as good or better shape than me. With the exception of Nature, who seemed to be getting her second wind and was continuing on to Canada after Katahdin, we all agreed that we were ready to wind this hike down. We were tired, but we all agreed that the Whites were something special and it would only get better. We were all eagerly looking forward to climbing Mt. Washington the next day.

The croo had to make a lot of food to feed 95 people and there were plenty of leftovers. The cook was a culinary student during the school year. The kid could cook. He made a pasta dish with wonderfully flavored pasta sauce that was out of this world. All of us filled our plates and went back for seconds. Featherfoot and I went back for thirds and fourths. There was a wonderful loaf of wheat bread that we used to mop up our plates. I was full. It broke my heart to see that we hadn't completely finished the pasta dish and the croo was going to throw the rest away.

I never was sick after gorging. My body very efficiently absorbed what it needed. A few times I heard hikers being sick after overeating. Featherfoot, Grits, and I washed the dishes for our work for stay. Lights were shut off at 9:30 pm and the guests headed to their bunks. Everyone turned on their headlamps and beams of light angled in all directions. I found a spot under a window to put my sleeping bag. It turned out to be a good choice. I saw clouds passing overhead and a sky full of stars before closing my eyes.

The dining room where we were sleeping was between the restrooms and the bunkrooms. With 95 guests, there was a continuous flow of people heading to the restrooms all night long. Each time the door to the bunk room opened it gave a loud creeeek and the wooden floor creaked as the person headed to the bathroom......................and back. Groan!

The next morning, Juice, Mama Llama, and Nature took off early. Featherfoot, Grits, and I stayed until the guests had gone and swept out the bunkrooms. After that we finished the leftovers from breakfast. There was a full pan of coffee cake and piles of pancakes with plenty of butter and syrup. As we were sitting in the dining area eating our pancakes, a heavy rainstorm came through. Rainwater was cascading off of the roof like a waterfall. I was glad to be sipping my coffee and watching this action and not hiking up the rocks of Mt. Washington like Juice, Mama Llama, and Nature. I talked to them at the top and they had gotten pounded.

13 MT. WASHINGTON

I had been reading about other hiker's adventures hiking Mt. Washington for the past three years. This could be a dangerous climb and descent and the weather could change in an instant. There could be snow on Mt. Washington every month of the year. Many people lost their lives. In fact, at the top, there was a building that had a snack bar and museum and a wall listing the names and dates of the people who died.

Over the years I developed a fantasy of what my hike over Mt. Washington would be like when it was my turn. I started to believe it. By the time I reached the base of Mt. Washington and after hiking over 1,800 miles, I would be in tremendous condition. I would start my hike at first light, whiz up the mountain, whiz down the other side, and hike thirty miles. People would be astounded!

"Wingo really hiked Mt. Washington and hiked thirty miles?"

"He sure did. The guy's an animal!"

If you turn back to the beginning of the book, I mentioned something about "reality colliding with dreams".

Sigh!

Featherfoot, Grits, and I started out together. I was leading. We hadn't gone fifty yards before I took a wrong turn. My navigational skills were already suspect after the Zealand Falls hut debacle. Featherfoot, who had hiked this area before, called out to me and I headed back to the right pathway. It looked like it was going to be a long day.

The climb from Lakes of the Clouds hut to the top of Mt. Washington was 1,276' in 1.4 miles. It was steep and rocky and it seemed like I passed every Lakes of the Clouds guest from the previous night. I was burning that huge sugary breakfast and it took about an hour to reach the top. I met Juice, Mama Llama, Featherfoot, and Slagline at the summit house. There was a snack bar where I bought a couple of hot chocolates and a steaming bowl of chili con carne with crackers.

Grits got lost and never did make it to the summit house. Juice and Mama Llama took the wrong trail and ended up next to the cog railway tracks before finding another route to the top. The Trail was not very well marked in this area and I wasn't the only one to make a mistake.

Featherfoot, Nature, and I headed out together. From the summit sign where everyone had their pictures taken, it was difficult to find the Trail leading down the mountain. We searched all over the place. Finally, Featherfoot suggested to Nature that they ask Wingo which way the Trail was.......... and head in the opposite direction. Grrr! My navigational skills were the brunt of too many jokes for the rest of my hike.

We finally found the Trail and about a quarter of a mile down, stopped and watched the cog train making its way up the steep hill. Hikers for many years had mooned the train but authorities were cracking down on that.

The weather was warm, sunny, and slightly breezy and it looked like it was going to be a beautiful day. I was wearing my short sleeved shirt and had my raincoat attached to the back of my pack. A little further along the Trail hikers were feeding a pair of wild birds. I don't know what they were, but they were as big as a blue jay. They were being fed sunflower seeds and were so tame they were landing on outstretched hands and arms. These birds had a good thing going and looked very healthy.

This was difficult hiking. Featherfoot and Nature were soon dots in the distance. Every inch of the day's hike was above tree line and over and around rocks of all sizes. After an hour of warm, sunny, hiking, the clouds started to move in. The Great Gulf Wilderness which was a vast valley with a lake at the bottom would go in and out of view. It started to drizzle lightly and the temperature dropped. I put on my raincoat and considered putting on my fleece pullover but decided I didn't need it yet. There were lots of climbs, descents, and rock scrambling. The rain was making the rocks slick.

As I was putting on my raincoat, a hiker caught up to me. He stopped and chatted. He was 73 years old and had started a ten day hike with twelve other people. He had one more day to go and the group was down to two people. The others had dropped out because of illness or injury and there were a number of injuries. I liked the man's spirit. While he was talking, he slipped twice on the slick rocks and both times fell down hard.

As I started to head up Mt. Jefferson, the wind began to pick up and I was hiking in fog. I hiked from cairn to cairn. The fog was so bad that I headed out from a cairn, got about twenty feet away, and couldn't find the next cairn in the distance. I glanced back to see if the cairn I just left was still visible. Just barely. I ventured a little further forward and saw the next cairn. Whew! Those cairns were truly life savers.

It was becoming less foggy but the wind was now blowing hard. Little ice pellets were blowing against my face and I had to duck my head into the wind. I would look up to get my bearings, squint as the wind and tiny ice particles stung my eyes, duck my head down again and move forward. My hands were extremely cold and becoming numb. As I neared the top, the wind was fierce. Gusts would hit my pack and push me to the side. As I moved forward I was leaning into the wind at such a steep angle I could practically touch the ground with my hands. I was working hard to climb the mountain but my body was getting cold. I wanted to stop and put on my pull over but thought that it would take too much time to dig out of the pack and I would lose too much body heat if I stopped. I knew I could not waver. I needed to keep moving forward and focus on getting to the hut. I fell down hard on a slippery rock and banged both hands breaking the fall. My hands were so numb I didn't feel any pain. That worried me. I moved each finger to make sure they were not broken. I could barely hold onto the hiking poles. I slipped again, got up, and slipped again.

I topped Mt. Jefferson, put my head down, and kept on grinding. My total concentration was on moving forward and making it to Madison Spring hut. I knew that I couldn't stop. I was very cold. I added numbers in my head to make sure I wasn't becoming hypothermic. I reached Thunderstorm Junction. A sign said that Madison Spring hut was a mile away. That gave me hope but I wasn't celebrating yet. In these conditions I knew it would take me well over an hour to get there.

A half an hour later the storm passed through, the sun began to shine, and my spirits picked up. To get to the hut there was a steep slippery descent over rocks. I could see the hut and kept saying to myself: "After all you've been through, don't break your neck now!" I arrived at the hut at 6:00 pm. It took all day to hike 7.1 miles.

I asked for work for stay and got it. They weren't turning anyone away this night. It was a small hut and filled to capacity with vacationers, so Featherfoot, Mama Llama, Juice, Slagline, Grits, Nature, and Zipper were outside when I arrived. They gave me a cheerful greeting.

Juice was talking to a vacationer and they looked at me when I walked by. Both of my legs were bloody. I had re-opened the wound under my knee and the blood had flowed down and stained my sock. I had a bloody arm and elbow. Juice looked at the vacationer and said: "That's a thru-hiker." She nodded in agreement.

I met Zipper for the first time on Mt. Jefferson just as the weather was starting to get bad. We were in a slippery area with steep drop-offs. The first thing she said to me was: "I'm Zipper. Glad to meet you. At least now I know there will be someone who will be able to identify my body." We talked a couple of minutes and then she zipped by. That lady never did anything in half measures.

The sun soon descended below the mountain, the breeze picked up, and it was cold. Juice took the initiative and we all headed to the bunk room to get out of the cold while the guests had their dinner. It felt good being out of the cold wind. As we were talking, I looked out of the window and saw a weasel. Everyone excitedly headed to the window and we watched it bounce around for a few minutes before it bounded back into the woods. That was fun.

I kept waiting for the 73 year old hiker to show up and breathed a sigh of relief when he came trudging in at 7:00 pm. There were 14 thru-hikers that night who stayed at the hut - seven NOBO's and seven SOBO's. We tried our best to stay out of the way of the guests. Some guests invited us to join them in conversation or cards, others were kind of irritated. This was a night to be inside the hut.

After dinner, the croo had enough food left over to feed all 14 of us. That was generous. I don't think they could have miscalculated the food requirements of their regular guests by that much. They had jobs for all 14 of us and that hut was probably cleaner and more organized than it had ever been. The food was good and I could feel my body regaining the heat that had been lost on the day's hike. That night, sleeping bags completely filled the small dining room. Hikers were sleeping on the floor and on top of all the dining room tables. I was in a corner beside a dining room table. Zipper was sleeping on top of the table and Featherfoot was on the other side. I slept surprisingly well. The bunkroom and bathrooms were closed to the dining room so we didn't have those distractions, plus I was exhausted from the day's hike.

Most of the hikers left early the next morning. I saw Nature, Juice, and Mama Llama take off together heading up Mt. Madison on a windy, cold morning. They started hiking for the first time as a group on this day. It would be another 250 miles before I would see them again.

I swept the dining area and had another filling breakfast. I was liking this. It was close to 10:00 am before I started out. One of the croo members was playing a flute quite beautifully. I listened to that sound as I climbed Mt. Madison. From what I heard, the wind was horrific early in the day and made for a memorable climb. When I started, it was a sunny, breezy, day and it was an enjoyable climb. The climb was above tree line and mainly big rocks and boulders. The cairns pointed the way and there was no set trail. I had to make my own decisions going up. It was a fun, challenging climb. On top of Mt. Madison, the views were incredible. I opened my tent and spread it out to let it dry while I had lunch. I was next to the imposing Mt. Washington and could see the mountains I had hiked the past few days. The Trail followed the spine of the mountain down to the bottom. It was a tricky descent. I used my hands instead of my hiking poles descending from rock to rock.

Just before I reached Pinkham Notch, I caught up to the 73 year old man and his hiking partner. This was their destination. They were both proud of their accomplishment and were elated. They asked me to take their picture and their faces were beaming.

I needed to get into Gorham, New Hampshire and replace my hiking boots and get some warmer clothes. My boots had only lasted 34 days and 403 miles and were ripped to shreds. This time I was more philosophical. The Trail was tough on boots. Buy some new ones. I decided to get some insulated rainwear. I bought a warm rain jacket and warm rain pants. I never used either of them for hiking but they were great to sleep in.

I was loyal to my little yellow, by now, "beat to shit" rain jacket. My sister gave it to me four years earlier and living in New Mexico it saw about four days of rain in that time. I used to feel guilty when I would open the closet and see it brightly shining on its hanger. I was loyal to my black swimming trunks that I bought at Walmart for $9. I wore them every day of my hike.

It was an eleven mile hitch into Gorham but the first car stopped for me. The man had thru-hiked three years earlier and his wife had been ground support. They were a couple in their sixties.

I decided to re-supply, go to the Outfitters for the boots and raingear, and spend the night at a motel. I stayed at the Gorham Motor Inn. It was a good, quiet, little motel on the far end of town.

When I was checking into the motel, I needed to decide if I was going to spend one night or two. There were two Wingo's who were constantly battling throughout the journey.

Wingo #1 was a competitive, driven, goal oriented, go-getter:

"I'm going to average 20 miles a day."

"I'm going to hike the Trail in four months."

"I haven't reached my mileage goal for the day. I need to hike into the night."

"I need to hike 10 hours a day............12 hours would be better."

"Break's over - back out into the rain!"

Wingo #2 was much more laid back. He wasn't listened to much at first, but became much more persuasive toward the end of the hike:

"You hiked fast the first part of your journey and have earned the luxury of hiking at a more relaxed pace. Slow down. Enjoy the experience."

"Your body is tired. You don't have to push it hard anymore. You can coast and still get to Katahdin long before your plane trip back to Albuquerque on October 5th."

"This is beautiful country you are hiking through. Enjoy it. Slow down."

I decided to spend two nights at the motel.

So far, hiking through the Whites had been fun, exhilarating, physically and emotionally exhausting, and I was drained. I took a long, hot shower, neosporined, taped my wounds, and headed to the Chinese all-you-can-eat restaurant next door. I was starving! The restaurant had a good reputation with thru-hikers. There was a huge selection of food. It cost $10. I was given a plate and I headed to the buffet. Each time I finished a plate, I picked up a new one. Six plates later, I had eaten about every item available. Mmmm. Mmmm. Mmmm.

The owner was saying something under her breath in Chinese when I went to pay. I probably didn't want to know what she was saying. I headed back to the motel and called Johanna and Bob, and Doug and Ingrid. Those phone calls always re-energized me. It was a quiet motel. The bed was soft and clean and I slept well.

It felt good to wake up at my usual time a little before 6:00 am, turn over and go back to sleep. I spent the day doing things at a leisurely pace. This was my first zero day other than when I stayed with my brother and sister. It felt great. I watched some TV that night and slept in late.

I headed back to the Trail at 10:00 the next morning. Fortunately, I got a quick hitch back to Pinkham Notch. The climb up Wildcat Mountain was a steep one. From the top, I could see Gorham in the distance. I passed some beautiful ponds. It was extremely difficult hiking and I reached Carter Notch by 3:00 pm. I had only hiked six miles and was drained. The next camping spot was Imp Shelter campsite which was six miles distant. Camping was only permitted at designated campsites in the Whites. I didn't think I could make it to the campsite before dark.

I asked for work for stay. The super nice croo leader said yes. She even had me taste test the chili she was making for dinner. I think anything would have tasted great, but I dipped my spoon into the chili, tasted it, closed my eyes thoughtfully and delivered my verdict: "Excellent!"

In their free time a lot of croo members hiked around the area. I was sitting outside chatting with one of them and he enthusiastically pointed to Carter Dome, 1,500' up the steep side of South Carter Mountain. It was on the Trail and I would be passing it the next morning. "Wingo, you've got some time before we need you at the hut. Carter's Dome has incredible views. You should go up there and check them out." Do you think I shared his enthusiasm?......................I don't think so.

This was the only hut that wasn't filled to capacity with vacationers. There were twelve paying customers. It was spread out. There was the main hut with the cooking and dining area and quarters for the croo, and there were two bunk buildings that looked fairly new. This was the last day of the season for the hut. Eventually three SOBO's showed up and were given work for stay. The dinner was excellent and as much as I could eat. We were going to sleep in the dining room but I think the croo wanted to celebrate their last night so we got to sleep in one of the empty bunkhouses.

The next morning after the guests had gone it was our time to have breakfast. There were piles of pancakes, bacon, and oatmeal. This will show you the difference between a starving NOBO with no body fat, and SOBO hikers who were just starting their journey. Two of the SOBO's were overweight and still feeding off of their body fat. They were full after a couple of pancakes. The other SOBO was skinny, but a finicky eater. He ate half of a cold pancake, looked like he had indigestion, and gave up. Since they weren't eating they were assigned cleaning the dishes. They were giving me dirty looks as I was eating breakfast. I had a gold mine of food in front of me and wasn't about to stop until I finished it all. I did, too.

I swept out the bunkhouses and the dining room before I left. I headed up to Carter Dome. The views were excellent. This was a day of heavy duty hiking. I hiked over four mountains before ending the day with a steep 3,000' descent to Rattle River shelter where I was going to spend the night. The remnants of Hurricane Danny were starting to show up and it was raining by the time I arrived. A group of troubled teens had the shelter spaces. It was the first day of their hike. They were novices. Even their leaders seemed like novices. It was getting dark and windy and looked like it was going to be a rough night. The worst part of the storm was predicted for the next day. It was 6:00 pm and only two miles to U.S. 2 and a three mile hitch into Gorham, New Hampshire. I opted for Gorham.

It turned out to be a rough night - at least as I observed it from my room at the Gorham Motor Inn. I always wondered how those kids weathered the night and the next day. I zeroed the next day, did some laundry, hit McDonalds for breakfast, hit an Italian restaurant for pizza, watched some TV, and watched the rain pouring all day - a perfect zero day. The town was packed with thru-hikers waiting out the storm. I didn't feel guilty. We were still in the Whites and those rocks were extra slippery and dangerous in the rain and heavy wind.

The next morning was bright and sunny as I headed back to the Trail. I hiked 12 miles on nasty, difficult, trail that passed serene ponds, streams, and thick forest made for moose. There were lots of moose droppings, some of them fresh, but I was getting discouraged. Maybe I wasn't going to see a moose. I ended the day camped next to Genetian Pond shelter. Tomorrow I would enter Maine. I took time to reflect on my hike through New Hampshire. Wow! What a state! What a fun, beautiful, challenging, state!

The first day in Maine was strenuous. I kept waiting for the Maine/New Hampshire marker to show up. When it finally did I couldn't help but smile. One more state to go!

Climbing Mt. Carlo I was passed by Stats for the first time. I felt like the tortoise to the hare with this guy. Almost all the way from here to Katahdin he was continuously shooting by me. He summited on September 20th. We always chatted when he caught up to me. I enjoyed his company. His was such a common story. When he started his thru-hike on March 14th he was forty pounds overweight. There is a picture on his Trail Journals site showing him jowly and beefy. He was in his early thirties. When he passed me, he was an efficient, conditioned, hiking machine.

By the time thru-hikers reached Maine the Trail had turned them into the most efficient hiking machines they could be. Excess weight was inefficient. By Maine even the hikers who had started fifty or more pounds overweight were now rail thin. It was always a shock to see a perfectly conditioned hiker and learn he had been fifty pounds overweight. For some reason the Trail took weight off of the shoulders. Before I started my hike I worked hard to build up my shoulders. I thought it would make it easier to carry my backpack. Within a month my shoulders were bony. All thru-hikers had bony shoulders. Fat was taken away from places where it wasn't needed. Faces had a gaunt look. Fat reserves were almost non-existent. The fat on my sides and lower back was completely burned off. Since I carried a 28 pound backpack for eight hours or more each day and had been for four months, what was left of my shoulders, sides, and lower back was hard muscle. The last time I remember having that low a percentage of body fat was when I was twelve years old. With that much activity and so little body fat I was constantly eating and consumed by thoughts of food.

There was so much hand over hand climbing, grabbing of branches and roots, stretching of legs and arms to pull myself up or lower myself down the rocks, that the hiking machine that was Wingo became strong and flexible. It was a wonderful feeling having all my muscles working together as I worked my way up or down a rock face. Every muscle was pulling its share of the load, particularly the core muscles from the lower chest to the upper pelvis. There was no lag time waiting for a weak stomach muscle to catch up. The Trail made my legs bigger, particularly my calves. They were challenged daily with punishing climbs and descents and they needed to be strong to handle it. I asked my brother, Doug, to take a picture of my calves when we were climbing Katahdin. I said they would never look like that again. He laughed but took a couple of shots to humor me.

By Maine, women thru-hikers had legs that were beautifully toned. They definitely should have had pictures taken. There was a trade-off, though. Their legs had scabs, scars, scratches, and nasty bug bites.

After months of climbing mountains the lungs became extremely efficient. If I was hiking up a steep mountain with other thru-hikers we could effortlessly have a conversation. It was jarring to pass day hikers on a climb and hear their labored breathing.

It's a nice memory. Wingo - the hiking machine.

At 4:00 pm I passed a tent on top of the East Peak of Goose Eye Mountain. It was right next to the ridge and was being pelted by the wind.

Someone had not done a good job of setting up the tent and it was flapping loudly. It struck me as odd that someone would put a tent so close to the ridge line, knowing that the wind speed would increase as it flowed over the ridge. I didn't want to intrude so I kept going. I reached Full Goose campsite and put up my tent on one of the platforms. I was the only person there. A mountain rescue team came hiking in about half an hour later. There were four of them. They had gotten a call from an injured hiker and didn't know his location. I thought about the tent flapping loosely in the wind and gave them the location. Within the hour a small spotter plane was circling Goose Eye Mountain.

14 MAHOOSUC NOTCH

The Mahoosuc Notch was on the agenda for the next day. This was one full mile of gnarliness that everyone looked forward to with as much anticipation as Mt. Washington, the rocks of Pennsylvania, the Shenandoahs, McAfee Knob, and the Smokies. It was one mile of boulders and rocks where you had to use your wits, physical skills, and imagination to get through.

It took a couple of hours to get to the notch after leaving Full Goose campsite, then I began the challenge I had been waiting for. I absolutely loved it! I would start up a boulder and have two or three options to get over it or around it. There were a couple of areas where boulders were leaning against one another and the pathway was through a tiny tunnel. I made it through the first tunnel by sliding on my stomach and didn't have to take off my pack. I had to take my pack off for the second tunnel and push it through the hole and follow it. It was harder than it sounds.

Some boulders were so steep that I focused on my footholds and handholds and didn't look down. A couple of times I had to pull my body up to a higher level just using the strength of my arms; like a pull-up with a 28 pound pack. It was one mile full of puzzle after puzzle. Sometimes it was downright scary, but doable, which made it fun.

Almost at the end there was a drop off that made me hesitate. Do you remember in cowboy movies where the cowboy is galloping on his horse and leaps over a narrow gorge with a drop off that looks like it goes down forever? That was the first thing that ran through my mind. The distance across was about five feet, and instead of forever the distance straight down was 20', but it was enough to make me wonder if I could do it. Should I take off my pack and try to sling it over to the other side? How much of a running start do I need? Can I even run with this pack? It took a couple of minutes to make a decision and when I was ready to go my adrenaline was pumping and my heart racing. I kept my pack on, took five fast steps, and leaped with everything I had! I landed solidly on the other side with not much room to spare. Man that was a good feeling! What a relief! I walked around with a bit of a swagger for a few minutes. It took two hours to complete the one mile Mahoosuc Notch and I enjoyed every minute of it!

Following the Mahoosuc Notch, the Mahoosuc Arm was almost as talked about. It went from 2,150' to 3,770' in 1.6 miles and was about the steepest continuous grade that I can remember. It didn't zig zag, it went straight up with lots of rock scrambling. My adrenaline was still pumping so hard from the Mahoosuc Notch that I didn't slow down until I hit the top. What a fun, fun, day.

I finished the 12 mile day at Bald Pate Lean-to. In Maine, shelters were called lean-to's. It was almost dark and it was chilly. Students from a nearby college had a good fire going and I enjoyed feeling its warmth. They offered to make a space for me in the shelter but I found a good spot to put my tent. They were backpacking for a week as part of their college orientation.

The next day started with a climb above tree line to Baldpate Mountain (West Peak) and another mile to Baldpate Mountain (East Peak). I thought that the rocky, difficult, hiking would get easier once I left New Hampshire. I was sadly mistaken. It didn't let up at all. On the way down East Baldpate I caught up to Slagline and Grits. They were planning to stay at a hostel when they reached East Hill Road in seven miles. Slagline had already called ahead and a driver from the hostel would be waiting for them at a pre-arranged time. I needed to re-supply so I decided to get a ride into town with them. The more I thought about it the better the idea of spending the night at the Pine Ellis Hiking Lodge sounded. It was in the little town of Andover, Maine. Within five minutes of the time we arrived at the road, David was there with his van and a half gallon container of cold lemonade.

When we reached the Lodge I put my gear in the bunkroom and headed to the Andover Grocery store and deli to re-supply and eat. The person next to me at the checkout counter was eying the twenty-four Snickers Bars I bought as part of my resupply. I told him they would last four days. He looked a little nauseous. I had a good double cheeseburger and fries. The person sitting next to me at the counter was not a hiker and left half of his dinner on his plate. I kept staring in disbelief at all those calories going to waste.

The next day was an enjoyable day of hiking. The temperatures were cool but pleasant. I could put in a lot of effort and not break a sweat. Reds, oranges, and yellows were starting to show on the trees. Maine was full of ponds of all sizes. Some were huge and should have been called lakes. I passed a couple on this day. They seemed to invite me to sit next to them and take a break. This was hard, rocky, climbing, where I worked for the miles. I climbed up Old Blue Mountain and hiked over toward the West Peak of Bemis Mountain. I was trying to get to the Bemis Mountain lean-to but ran out of daylight. Before the summit of Bemis Mountain, I found a spot right next to the Trail just big enough to put my tent. In Maine, the trees were close together and it was hardly ever flat so it was next to impossible to find a place to put a tent. Trail maintainers would occasionally make an emergency space in case a hiker couldn't make it to a lean-to. This was where I put my tent. I had my headlamp on as I put my ground cloth and tent over a soft covering of leaves. It was cool enough that I could see my breath in the lamplight. After a hard day of hiking the coolness felt good. I brought out my food bag and was sitting on the Trail making a couple of peanut butter and jelly on cinnamon bagel sandwiches when Stats hiked by. We chatted and I could see him looking for a place to put his tent. There wasn't one and he headed on to the Bemis Mountain lean-to. I turned off my headlamp and ate my sandwiches by the light of the stars while listening to the sounds of the night.

I started finding places to pull off at night in Maine and loved it. Because of the heavy load of hikers in New Hampshire and Vermont, the ATC discouraged staying anywhere but in shelters or campsites. In Maine, there were gorgeous areas where I could tent alone. It all came together in Maine. I found the right mixture of being around people during the day and enjoying the solitude and quiet of the outdoors at night. A number of nights I still camped with other people but I treasured those nights alone.

I only hiked ten miles the next day and it wasn't a difficult day for hiking. I was finally slowing down my hike and enjoying it. There was very little elevation change during the hike and I hiked alongside two large ponds for at least three miles. One pond was a vacation spot with sailboats and motorboats. The other was more primitive.

In the afternoon as I was walking beside the primitive pond I saw my first moose! It was a female and was grazing 30' to the left of the Trail. I was expecting big, but I wasn't expecting That Big! Wow! She saw me but wasn't bothered by me. I was hoping another hiker would come by but it didn't happen and after a while I hiked on. Five minutes later and 30' to my left, she galloped by as fast and as smoothly as a horse. My first moose sighting! I was pumped! I had been hoping for this from the beginning of my hike.

I reached Sabbath Day Pond lean-to a half an hour later and was dying to tell someone of my moose sighting. Nobody was there. I set up my tent in an area of spruce, pines, and maples. My tent was thirty yards from Sabbath Day Pond. Large shady trees surrounded the pond. Big rocks were spaced around the pond, some even in the water. Sabbath Day Pond was the recommended water source for hikers. I still had 32 ounces of water and wasn't about to use it as a water source. I sat around hoping someone would show up...and waited...and waited. Finally it was dark and I called it a night.

The next morning as I was taking down my tent I started hearing tree branches moving loudly and occasionally snapping. This would last a few seconds and stop. In a minute or two the sound of moving branches would start again, last a few seconds, and stop. I pin pointed the sound which was between me and the pond. All of a sudden an absolutely huge silhouette of a moose loomed from the trees. It was practically as tall as the small trees surrounding it. It was so out of proportion that it was startling. I quietly walked closer to get an even better look. The moose slowly headed to the pond. I followed. She casually entered the pond and walked up to her knees in the water. I found a spot on a rock twenty feet away and watched.

She would plunge her massive head into the water and bring up plants in her mouth. Parts of the plants would be hanging loosely from her mouth as she chewed. Water dripped from the plants and rippled on the still, quiet pond. Sometimes she would put her face in the water and blow bubbles. Being so close, I was awed by her size. Eventually she headed back to land and I reluctantly headed back, too.

I passed another beautiful pond surrounded by tall trees. There were places that would have been perfect camping spots but it was too early. It was hot summer when I started hiking the White Mountains in New Hampshire. I was so focused on getting through them in one piece that when I reached Maine my mind finally registered that the leaves were starting to change color and the temperatures were cooling.

It was early September. In the mountains it was beginning to feel like fall - at least from a New Mexican's perspective. I only hiked 11miles on a relatively easy hiking day and I spent a lot of the time enjoying the beauty of my surroundings. The next day the Trail slapped me in the face and brought me back to reality. I think if I had seen a map profile of this day's hike with its long, steep ups and equally long, steep downs - mountain after mountain - I would have said "Forget it!"

It had a little bit of everything. I passed ponds, forded streams, walked on wooden planks over swampy bogs, and climbed a lot of rocks. Much of the time was spent above tree line. On top of Saddleback Mountain at 4,120' I noticed for the first time one of the things that made Maine my favorite state. There was forest as far as I could see in any direction and it stayed that way to the end of my hike. I could see tiny towns and small roads in the distance; but that was about it as far as signs of civilization. In Maine, I felt like I was in wilderness.

I hiked 15 rugged miles and found another emergency camping spot to put my tent near the top of Lone Mountain. I had an hour of daylight left and knew that I wouldn't be able to make it to Spaulding Mountain lean-to before dark. Hell, to be honest, I was liking these emergency pull-offs. After talking with Car Hop ten minutes earlier, I knew the Spaulding Mountain lean-to was crowded with people.

I had first seen Car Hop when he scared the heck out of me on top of Shenandoah Mountain in New York at 1:00 in the morning. We passed each other at least fifteen more times during our thru-hikes. He was my source of information for what was ahead on the Trail. He let me know how close I was to the next shelter, how many people were at the shelter, and who was ahead of me. He enjoyed chatting and was more than happy to answer all my questions.

Car Hop's hike was unusual. He was in his early fifties, fit, and had lost a lot of weight. He lived in Bethesda, Maryland with a wife and two teen-aged children. As he was hiking the Trail he was working full time. He was self-employed and able to do his job using his phone and computer. Once in a while he would be off the Trail for a few days when he would fly home and meet with his client. He was one of those people who only needed about four hours of sleep a night. He said that he couldn't sleep more than six hours if he tried.

He was a North bound hiker heading toward Katahdin who hiked South each day. He had two cars and at 5:00 pm would drive one car north to a trailhead and hike south until one or two in the morning until he reached his other car. He would then drive to a motel, sleep for four hours, have breakfast, work until 5:00 pm, get into his car, head north to the next trailhead, and repeat the process all the way to Katahdin. His cars continually leapfrogged all the way to Katahdin. He always hiked in shorts, sandals, shirtless, with a tiny daypack, hiking poles, and his headlamp. He was deep into Maine before he made concessions to the weather. He added a t-shirt and socks.

This was moose country if I had ever seen it. The trees were tightly spaced and the ground cover was moss, with lots of spruce trees. There were small bushes here and there. I put my tent on a level spot three feet from the Trail. After putting up my tent, there was enough light, so I walked around and checked out the area. I noticed there might have been a pathway leading down the mountain that passed right over the spot I had put my tent. It was long ago because it had blended back into the forest, but it looked like an old pathway to me.

This felt like real backpacking: Being alone, high on a mountain, away from cell phones, or any other distractions. Breathing deeply the fresh, clean, mountain air and feeling an inner calmness and quiet. Seeing stars peeking through the tall trees. Feeling the coolness of the first signs of fall. Listening to night sounds. I got into my sleeping bag. It was peaceful and quiet. I had a feeling I would sleep well. I closed my eyes. Almost immediately I heard a sound I had never heard before. A small animal would zip by my tent. I must have been next to its nightly route. It would zip the other way. Pretty soon it would zip by again. It moved fast and seemed to bound. It occasionally made a buzzing sound. After a while it noticed me. It stopped and I could sense it getting ready to check out the new occupant. I had my boots under the overhang of my tent. It zipped right toward them and aggressively started pulling on a boot. I whapped the side of the tent and it shot away. It stood away from the tent making its zzz zzz zzz sound. I had a feeling it was cussing me out. It came bounding by many more times in the night but never bothered me after that. I'm not sure what it was. Maybe a weasel?

I closed my eyes and waited for sleep. I must have been on an animal thru- way. By now I knew what a moose sounded like. Snap, crack, crack, crunch, pop. One was heading my way! Snap, Pop, Crack, Crack, Snap. By now I knew how HUGE those animals were! SNAP, CRACK, SNAP, POP, CRACK. I had heard that they could be aggressive - particularly bull moose. SNAP! CRACK! POP! SNAP! CRACK! I remembered Bronco telling about a moose he had startled that ran headlong into a tree. The memory was not filling me with confidence. SNAP!! CRACK!! POP!! SNAP!! CRACK!! CRACK!! My anxiety level was doubling, tripling, quadrupling! Would it even see my tiny tent - and my tent was feeling mighty tiny - before stepping on it? ON ME?? CLICK!! CLICK!! CLICK!! CLICK!! Oh shit! It's on the rocky Trail! What do I do now? I don't want to startle it because it could run right over me.

I quietly turned on my headlamp. It made a startled jump when it saw the light. I quickly unzipped my tent. By the time I got out I could hear its hooves clicking swiftly along the rocky Trail and it was out of sight. I was all wound up! I got back into my sleeping bag but didn't even try to go back to sleep. I inhaled deeply and exhaled slowly a few times and listened to the sounds of the night. Soon, I was sound asleep.

I awoke the next morning at dawn. The forest was quiet and peaceful as I took down my tent and loaded my pack for the day's hike. I accidentally left my sham wow cleaning cloth at this camping spot. It had loyally done its job for four months. It looked pathetic. It had blood stains on it, deeply embedded dirt stains, and holes all over it. I was truly saddened when I realized it was gone. It had earned a completion of the journey and retirement. I had a Pop Tart before I started hiking. The Spaulding Mountain lean-to was only two miles away where I planned to cook a hot breakfast.

I arrived at the lean-to as everyone was getting up and getting ready for the day. It was Sunday, September 6th, Labor Day weekend. The lean-to and surrounding campsites were packed. A lot of hikers were out for the weekend. Blue Ray was at the lean-to. It was good seeing him again. I hadn't seen him since early Pennsylvania. Joe Kick Ass was there. I met a couple of thru-hikers for the first time who were hiking with Blue Ray.

It was an interesting dynamic. There were five thru-hikers and ten weekend/section hikers. Blue Ray and his hiking buddies had spent the night in the lean-to and were not too pleased. They kept mentioning loudly, how they weren't able to sleep because: "Those fucking Day Hikers kept Zipping and Unzipping their FUCKING SLEEPING BAGS all night long!" (If it hadn't been sleeping bags it would have been something else.) The other hikers were hearing this and looked guilty, almost remorseful.

This is hard to explain, but by the time thru-hikers reached Maine, they had achieved a status with other hikers. When I arrived at the lean-to, I sat next to the fire ring, took out my stove and started boiling water to make a hot meal. I was soon joined by the other thru-hikers. As we made our breakfast, we chatted and joked. There was a camaraderie, a cockiness, a feeling of shared adventure that set us apart. None of the other hikers intruded in our space. My natural inclination was to include all hikers and I didn't like the idea of intimidating other hikers, but just for this breakfast - this one fleeting moment- I enjoyed being part of this exclusive group.

It was an extremely challenging day of hiking. Up Spaulding Mountain (4,000'), down to the Carrabassett River (2,100') and a challenging ford. Up to South Crocker Mountain (4,040') and over to North Crocker Mountain (4,228'), then down to Maine Hwy 27 (1,450'), and a five mile hitch into Stratton, Maine.

My guess is that very few thru-hikers would name Stratton as their favorite Trail town. It was mine. I think it was because of a wonderful attitude and honesty. I was given a quick hitch by the ridge runner who was overseeing the Horn Pond lean-to and was re-supplying. I told him I was going to stay the night in Stratton and he told me the lady to talk to was Susan Smith, the owner of the Stratton Motel and Hostel. He dropped me off in front of her motel. I entered the office and she had a pot roast cooking that made my mouth water. It was Labor Day weekend and her motel was full. She could see my disappointment and said: "Let me make a couple of phone calls." She called the Spillover Motel and talked to the owner. "I've got a thru-hiker here who needs a room. Do you have one available? Good. You will give him the rate we agreed on? Good." She gave me a nice smile and directions and I was on my way.

The Spillover Motel was by far the best motel I stayed in during my thru- hike. It smelled fresh and new. Everything was fresh and clean. There was even a mint on my pillow. Talk about stepping up in the world. The rate I paid really was less than the standard rate. It had a bath tub that actually worked. I filled it almost to the top with water that was so hot I could barely get into it. I lay in that tub for half an hour washing dirt out of stubborn areas and massaging aching muscles in the hot soothing water. It was pure pleasure!

I went to the Stratton Diner for dinner and while I was waiting for my food, Susan Smith came by for some coffee. She asked if I had checked in at the Spillover Motel and if everything was all right. I thanked her and said everything was great. She asked me how I was enjoying my thru-hike and looked me in the eye while she waited for my answer. She really wanted to know. She dealt with thru-hikers every day. They were her thru-hikers. She really cared! She did it in an understated way which made it even better.

The next morning I had a continental breakfast of yogurt, blueberry bagels, and excellent coffee. The motel owner asked me how I liked my stay and acted like she wanted to know. I headed to Fotter's Market to re-supply. A couple in their fifties were the owners of this well stocked, prosperous looking, grocery store with its deli and wine racks. The owners knew what hikers used for backpacking and had those items in abundance. They could have gouged us. These honest owners had specials on almost all the items that I purchased. I had an excellent re-supply and smiled ear to ear when I saw the total. Susan's assistant gave me a free ride back to the Trail.

It was noon when I started hiking again. I only had 5.1 miles to get to Horns Pond lean-to so I didn't push the pace. There was more climbing than I had expected and I could feel the weight of the re-supply. There was a very steep rocky descent to Horns Pond and Horns Pond lean- to. I should have been paying attention but I was only a couple of hundred feet from the bottom and trying to see the pond and lean-to through the trees. I should have waited until I had my hiking poles firmly planted before moving forward but I was distracted. My right pole was the first to slide. I tried to stab it back into the ground but my body was leaning forward and it was too late. My left pole could not stop my momentum and both poles quickly slid behind me. The fall I'm about to describe scared the daylights out of me, even long after it happened.

I had on my fully re-supplied heavy pack and my body was falling head first down a very steep part of the Trail. I looked down to the area where I was going to land and it was nothing but rocks - some the size of a computer. I was heading face first toward a big rock and my heavy pack was pushing my head down so rapidly that my feet were lifted up into the air. I was within a millisecond of tumbling. I can't tell you exactly what happened next. It was reflexes and survival instinct. I rolled to my side before impact and my head missed the rock but I was falling so fast I knew there was going to be major damage when I hit. My right hand and right hip hit the rocks almost simultaneously. My right hip banged hard on a rock and took the major impact. The momentum of the fall kept me bouncing and sliding over rocks for another five feet. I banged my shins, knees, and elbows. The hip bone should have shattered. I touched it tentatively. It hurt like hell but it didn't feel broken. I took a few tentative steps and it held my weight. The impact should have broken some fingers, too. I couldn't believe my luck! The rocks roughed up and ripped open the flesh on my right hand, right elbow, all around the right knee, and my right and left shin. I have scars on my right hand, right elbow, and right leg that are permanent. I was a bloody mess and badly shaken. The only thing that kept going over and over in my mind was how incredibly lucky I was. By the time the fall ended, my hiking poles were twenty feet up the Trail. I didn't even try to patch things up. I let the blood flow, limped to the lean-to, and found a campsite. Fortunately, no one was there. I didn't want to be talking to anybody.

I found an isolated, flat spot to put my tent and did some major cleaning and bandaging. While I was cleaning and patching, I was trying to piece together what went wrong and how I could keep it from happening again. The conclusion was to make sure my poles were firmly planted before moving forward on steep descents and to stay focused. I had seen so many of those rocky, steep, descents by the time I reached Maine that I had lost the healthy respect I had for them in the beginning. They had my full respect to the end of my hike. When I made dinner that night I was facing Bigelow Mountain. I saw a fantastic sunset and breathed a huge sigh of relief my hike wasn't over.

I was a little shaky when I started out the next morning. I looked like the walking wounded. Within an hour of hiking, I was feeling fine. This day was hard climbing. A lot of it was above tree line in the Bigelows - West Bigelow, Avery Peak, and Little Bigelow Mountain. From above tree line there were views of many lakes and ponds surrounded by forest. It was an ideal day for hiking and I almost hated to come down, but eventually I headed to Little Bigelow lean-to to spend the night.

The next day was a pure delight. I hiked next to Flagstaff Lake which was huge. I could see little sailboats way in the distance. It was breezy and there were whitecaps on the water. I passed many ponds. Most ponds didn't have any signs of human activity. They were as primitive and pristine as they had been for thousands of years. One of them had a little beach where I sat in the sand and had some trail mix. A couple of the ponds were swampy, with plant life on the surface, dead tree trunks sticking out of the water, and a swamp like smell. Most were surrounded by tall trees that reflected off the water and created a tranquil setting. Hiking around ponds always gave me a strong feeling of being in the wilderness and glad to be there. There was very little elevation change during the 17 mile hike. The weather was sunny and breezy, and fittingly, I ended the day at Pierce Pond lean-to beside a lovely pond. There were loons in the pond. Well into the night I listened to them calling to one another.

The loons were even busier the next morning. I don't think I could have slept in if I had wanted to. My goal this day was to ford the Kennebec River. I was low on water and a mile into the hike there was a sign that said water was available at Harrison's Pierce Pond Camp .2 miles off the Trail. Harrison's Camp was an old lodge with a spacious living/dining room. The lodge had a picture window from floor to ceiling that looked out to a gorgeous setting of colorful maples, tall pines, and a meandering stream. Tim Harrison greeted me warmly and even though I only needed water, maintained that warmth. He pulled the water bottles out of the side of my backpack so I didn't have to take the pack off. He filled the water bottles and put them back in the pack. He told me the water was the "best tasting water in the world". I remember thinking: "What a beautiful lodge and gracious host. If I am ever back in this area, I would love to spend some time there." He had been in business for many years. The lodge was rustic but looked prosperous.

I hiked another hour and made it to the Kennebec River. This was a wide, swiftly flowing river. A canoe with a certified Maine guide was waiting to transport me across. The canoe had a white blaze painted on the floor. It was the official Appalachian Trail pathway. David took my pack and put it in the center of the canoe. He had me get in front and handed me a paddle. He sat in the rear of the canoe. He headed directly upstream for 100 feet. Toward the center of the river the rapidly flowing water looked fairly deep. David said it was shoulder deep. There was a hydro-electric plant upstream that let out a flow of water at unpredictable times. Sometimes the water was shoulder level, sometimes it was waist deep. David told me that every year there were cocky thru-hikers who would attempt to cross the river on foot. He said he had seen a number of them come close to drowning. One had drowned a few years back. I wouldn't have considered trying it but I heard that One Step and Fat Kid successfully crossed it four days later. When we reached the other side, I chatted with David while he was waiting for hikers to show up. He had a heavy Maine accent. It was so heavy I thought he might be putting it on to create the image of the "Maine guide" for the hikers. As he was enthusiastically telling about the swarms of mosquitoes and the hapless SOBO's I mentioned earlier, his Maine accent became even thicker. He was the real deal.

I had another hour of hiking to get to U.S. 201 and a hitch into Caratunk, Maine. I was dying to phone my brother and sister and say: "Hi. I'm in Caratunk, Maine". Unfortunately it was a long hitch and Wingo #1 was anxious to make some miles.

I hiked through beautiful, healthy, forest and followed a long pond where the pathway took me down to pond level, then up a couple of hundred feet, then down to pond level again, over and over, like a roller coaster. I caught up to La La and Frenchy who were taking a break on top of Pleasant Pond Mountain. La La were a young French couple who were charming and very verbal. Hence, the Trail name------La La La La La------ talks a lot. Their English was excellent but as a group they spoke to each other in French. Frenchy was the same age and Canadian. Since hikers mainly heard him speaking French, that's how he got his Trail name. They started their thru-hike in the middle of May and were fit and fast. They passed me a couple of times after a break and I could hear them coming long before they reached me.

As we began to descend Pleasant Pond Mountain we were walking together. They were a friendly group and wanted to talk. The descent was rocky and steep. I was using my hiking poles and grateful to have them. Female La was fifty feet ahead. Male La was just ahead of me. Frenchy was behind. Male La had on tennis shorts and he casually had his hands in his pockets as he stepped down the steep, rocky, pathway. It was amazing to watch his agility. When he was trying to make a point while conversing, he would keep his hands in his pockets, look back up at me, and continue the conversation. If he started to slip, he would quickly look forward, grab a nearby tree, steady himself, and not miss a step or beat in the conversation. As I watched in alarm as he nonchalantly averted fall after fall, I felt like a stressed, overworked, air traffic controller: "Yikes! Watch out! Watch out!" They were much faster so I let them go ahead. I don't think my frazzled nerves could have taken much more of them.

I hiked 19 miles and ended the day at a great campsite. I was camped next to a river. My tent was on a smooth level area resting on pine needles. I was surrounded by tall pine trees. I was in a narrow canyon and the sound of the swiftly flowing water was loud. There was a waterfall fifty feet downstream and I could see the water cascading over the falls and hear it crashing below. It wasn't a soothing sound. It was jarring until I got used to it. I set up camp, had dinner, watched the day turn to night, and fell asleep in the peaceful serenity of the great outdoors. Maine was about feelings, emotions. I loved Maine!

The next day I made my first serious river ford. There was a rope strung across the Piscataquis River. I shortened my hiking poles and stuck them on the back of my pack. I was glad to have the rope. The water was soon to the bottom of my shorts. Holding tightly to the overhead rope and moving hand over hand, I still had a hard time keeping my balance. The water was trying to get me and almost did a couple of times. I'm glad no one was around because I would have provided a lot of entertainment. I finally made it to the other side and my boots squished for the next half hour.

For the next hour I paralleled a large pond. The winds picked up, and there were large white caps on the water. I was holding onto my baseball hat to keep it from blowing away. Finally I turned it around with the bill facing backwards. A small motorized fishing boat was having a hard time of it; bobbing its way through the choppy water. I ended the day at Horseshoe

Canyon lean-to.

I was on the move early the next morning and had a nine mile hike to Monson, Maine. Monson was the re-supply town before entering the 100 Mile Wilderness. This was the last town before Katahdin. I needed nine days of food to make it through the 100 Mile Wilderness. Knowing my appetite, I knew I would be carrying a Heavy pack. I called my brother and finalized the time I would meet him at Katahdin Stream Campground. Doug was going to climb Katahdin with me.

I hiked three miles after leaving Monson and entered the 100 Mile Wilderness. It was the 12th of September and I was going to meet Doug on the 21st. That gave me ten days to hike 100 miles.

I remembered sitting around the campfire and listening to Robo talk about the 100 Mile Wilderness. He had thru-hiked the AT a few years earlier. We had been camped by a tiny pond in Virginia, two days before a visit with my sister. The man had a way with words. When he talked about the 100 Mile Wilderness he made it sound exciting and his voice was brimming with emotion. When he ended his talk he was looking at me and almost pleaded: "When you get to the 100 Mile Wilderness, slow down and enjoy it." By the time I reached the 100 Mile Wilderness I had hiked over halfway through Maine and was loving this state. I knew I would follow Robo's advice and take it slow.

I had enough food to get through the Wilderness and I hadn't had that much weight on my back since the Shenendoahs. My shoulders were killing me! The hike started with beautiful ponds and forests and I made it to Leemon Brook lean-to just before dark. I found a level spot thirty yards from the lean-to to put my tent. I was glad to have the pack off.

This far into the hike my body was hanging in there, but it was ready for the hike to end. I tried to help it out. Starting in Maine, with a few exceptions where I hiked into the night, I would end each day by 5:00 pm. That gave me more time to set up camp and relax. I went to bed at 8:00 pm and slept until 6:00 am - 10 hours of sleep. My sleep was erratic and I tossed and turned all night. Spending ten hours a night in bed helped make up for the lack of quality sleep. I didn't have any body fat. I was all bones and muscle. I slept on my side, so that if I was on my left side I could feel the weight of my body on the bones and muscles of that side and it made them ache. I could only stay in one position for a short period of time before I had to turn. By this time, both of my legs would kick spastically when I was in my sleeping bag. Sometimes I would feel a leg kick coming but couldn't do anything about it. Other times the leg would just kick. Before going to sleep, the legs would kick over and over. Often, just when I had gotten to sleep, a leg would kick and wake me up. My feet would cramp at night and I would have to spend time massaging them. Sometimes my foot, ankle, and lower leg would cramp at the same time. That was painful and would take a lot of massaging to loosen up.

My hands were strong and had calluses where I gripped my hiking poles. They ached at night from gripping the hiking poles all day. The muscles in my arms were hard and strong but they also ached from so much use. My neck and back ached. My shoulders ached 24 hours a day. I thought that as my thru-hike progressed I would get used to the weight of my pack and by the end of my hike would hardly notice it. Other hikers had said that in their journals. Bull Shit! It never got lighter. I was constantly shifting my shoulder straps to different areas of my shoulders while hiking to relieve the ache. My aching shoulders were even more of a nuisance toward the end of my hike.

I knew that by this time aspirin would have helped. I didn't have any or buy any. I wanted to be able to evaluate the degree of pain, so I didn't mask it. I was very lucky. I never had to take a day off because of injury or illness. This far into the hike everyone had aches and pains. They were part of the hike and hardly ever mentioned.

A couple of times I watched Jumar settle in for the night. He looked bone weary, almost feeble. He looked sooooo tired. He would groan as he made tighter and tighter circles before plopping down with a long loud siiiiiiigh. Sir Lawrence Olivier couldn't have portrayed "tired" better than Jumar. The next morning you wouldn't know it was the same dog. He was lively and eager to go. I think that would be a good description of me.

The next day was hiking that you dream about. The terrain was gentle and between 600' and 1,000'. The forest was full of maple trees and the leaves were starting to change color. There were golds, browns, yellows, oranges, reds, and many shades of green. Some leaves had fallen to the ground and the pathway was colorful. I passed North Pond and Little Wilson Falls. I rock hopped across Little Wilson Stream and plunged through knee deep water crossing Big Wilson Stream. Toward the end of the day the water was almost to my knees crossing Long Pond Stream. When I reached the other side I found a beautiful spot next to the stream that was twenty feet from the Trail. It looked ideal for camping. It had a smooth, level, surface, and was just the right distance from the stream so the flowing water made a soothing background sound. It was only 4:00 pm. Should I stay or keep going?

The once commanding voice of Wingo #1 was now tinny, weak, and bitter, but he gave it his best shot:

"Our goal is Long Pond Stream lean-to. Remember goals? It's only a mile. We can get there in less than an hour."

Wingo #2 chimed in: "This location is perfect. You only need to average ten miles a day and you've already gone eleven. You can sit here, relax, make yourself some dinner, and enjoy the sights and sounds. Your body will thank you for it."

Wingo #2 was sounding pretty persuasive.

Wingo #1 could sense defeat and became quarrelsome: "You don't listen to me anymore! I don't know why I bother!"

He sullenly headed back into the recesses of my mind and pretty much stayed there for the rest of my hike, although he did spend time reliving past glories:

"Remember when I hiked 227 miles in 11 days and got to my sisters a day early? And Bob said: 'We weren't expecting you until tomorrow.' "

"Remember when I hiked 41 miles?"

"Remember how surprised Cargen and Katz were when I passed them on that steep uphill climb?"   "Yep. Yep. Yep. Those were the days….."

I spent a lovely night beside the stream in a perfect camping spot, absorbing the beauty of my surroundings, and feeling it uplift my soul.

I was having breakfast at 7:00 the next morning and wasn't expecting to see anyone on the Trail that early when I heard people fording the stream. It was Juice, Mama Llama, and Nature. What a pleasant surprise. We had traveled over 250 miles since we had last been together. We chatted for a while and they headed on. This day and the next were Maine at its best. At times, the hiking was difficult with six mountains to climb. There were a lot of challenging, near vertical, rock climbs and descents. There were long wide rock slabs where I tacked side to side to get my best footing. The ground cover was a tight, velvety, moss with soothing shades of green. The trees were closely spaced and I wondered how a bull moose with its big antlers could maneuver, or what would happen if it panicked and started running in that dense forest. Moose droppings were everywhere. There was another challenging ford where I did my Rambo bit - hand over hand using an overhead rope. There was a small pond surrounded by birch trees with their white trunks and branches. It was like a pastel painting with many shades of soft color. I could feel my pupils dilate as they absorbed the greens, oranges, yellows, reds, and the light blue of the pond.

I ended the day near the top of White Cap Mountain. I put my tent in a little emergency pull-off spot. It was out of the direct wind but it was windy and cold. From the beginning of my thru-hike I had worried about not being able to handle the cold when I reached Maine. This was the test. It was September 16th. I was high on a mountain. A cold wind was blowing. It was cold when I got into my sleeping bag and it stayed windy and cold. I was toasty warm all night long in my 20 degree sleeping bag, insulated rainwear, two pair of socks, and gloves.

By this time I had spent so much time outdoors, my body had gotten used to the variations in temperature. On cold days it was uncomfortable to go into a restaurant or any other place where the temperature was 72 degrees or warmer. My cheeks would turn a ruddy color and be hot to the touch. I never put on long pants for hiking. I didn't need them. I would see other hikers all bundled up around the campfire looking cold, and I wasn't. I was pleasantly surprised that my body adapted to the cold as well as it did.

I started out early the next morning and was on top of White Cap Mountain when Juice, Mama Llama, and Nature caught up. We had 360 degree views of forests, ponds, lakes, and mountains. Juice got out his map. There was a tall mountain in the distance. We all debated whether or not it was Katahdin. Katahdin was still 73 miles away and that mountain looked a lot closer. I said that it wasn't. I think Mama Llama and Nature were starting to side with me. Juice re-oriented his map, pointing out features to the east and west and determined that it had to be Katahdin. He convinced us. It was our first glimpse of the mountain we had hiked 2,105 miles to see. It dwarfed all the surrounding mountains. I couldn't believe it could be that far away and that big. Just seeing my goal in sight for the first time energized me. We were all excited! White Cap Mountain at 3,650' was the highest mountain until we reached Katahdin. The hiking was still challenging to the end of the journey but there weren't any more long steep climbs until Katahdin.

As I approached the east branch of the Pleasant River I caught up to a backlog of hikers crossing the 100' wide river by stepping from rock to rock. It was a winding course and took each hiker between five and ten minutes. I took out my trail mix, found a comfortable spot to sit down, and enjoyed the action. It was entertaining. Kind of like watching a high wire act, with legs jutting to the side and arms circling for balance. One of the hikers took a spill and was razzed mercilessly by the other hikers. I let them finish and continue on, and then waded straight across. It took less than a minute and wasn't even up to my knees. Hikers had such a phobia about getting their boots wet. I never could understand it.

I ended the day at Crawford Pond. There was still plenty of daylight. It was big enough to be a lake. I was tented 30' from the water. There was a sandy beach. There were loons nearby making loud, clear, calls.

At the end of a hiking day I always enjoyed putting up my tent. I put it up at a leisurely pace. It was a good way to relax, unwind from the day's hike, and get comfortable with my surroundings. Some nights were busy nights for animal activity. This was one of them. The weasel was active with its quick bounding and zzz zzz zzz sound. I brought my boots into the tent. There was the sound of a larger animal at one point in the night. It wasn't a moose but it could have been a deer or bear. A slow moving porcupine took forever to get out of my area. The loons were calling far into the night. Wingo had dark bags under his eyes the next morning. Groan.

There was hardly any elevation change the next day. It was fun hiking around ponds and Jo-Mary Lake. I passed Pemadumcook Lake and ended the day at the Nahmakanta Stream campsite. It was a chilly night and Holmes and Watson had a good fire going at their campsite. Holmes was a nice young woman, section hiking from Pennsylvania with her hound dog - Watson. He was a great howler. We started leapfrogging at the start of the 100 Mile Wilderness and I could always tell when they were catching up to me. I visited a while and warmed my hands by the fire.

There were more lakes, streams, and ponds the next day. I was enjoying hiking in Maine and was having mixed feelings about my journey ending. My body was saying: "It's time." My mind was saying: "You've finally got the hang of it. You've found the right combination of being around people and being alone." I didn't want it to end, and yet, I did.

I camped that night at the Rainbow Lake campsite within 10' of the water. I could hear it lapping on the shore before I fell asleep. I camped with Nature, Juice, Mama Llama, and Jeff and Penny who were friends of Juice and Mama Llama. We sat next to our stoves, which whistled at different pitches, as we cooked our dinners and reminisced about our journey.

There was a climb the next morning to Rainbow Ledges. There were huge flat rock slabs and an incredible view of Katahdin. It loomed majestically in front of me. At 4:00 pm I crossed Abol Bridge. There was a gorgeous view of Katahdin from the bridge. Next to the bridge was the Abol Bridge campground where I spent the night.

I went to the camp store to get a camping spot and get some food. I ate a day's worth of food while talking to the young, blond, attractive, clerk. I was standing at the far end of the small store and a couple of people came in. As the clerk was talking to them, I heard her say: "By the time men thru-hikers reach this campground, they have these gigantic calves." She was staring at my calves as she said this. She made my day, I can tell you!

The campground had showers and it felt good to be clean and freshly shaved. I didn't sleep that great that night. I was too excited. I would be meeting Doug the next day, and the day after, we would be climbing Katahdin. I was up bright and early the next morning. Within a mile of the campground I entered Baxter State Park. This park had it all. I passed beautiful streams, rustic ponds, a big waterfall, and trees with brightly colored leaves. I passed bogs that were covered by long wooden planks. The weather in this area was harsh in the winter and a lot of the slick wobbly planks were almost completely rotten. I thought to myself: "Wouldn't it be great if I broke a leg right here?"

I was super cautious and made it to the Katahdin Stream campground by 1:00 pm. I checked in at the ranger station, got my permit to climb Katahdin the next day, was given a campsite, filled in my last shelter journal entry at the ranger station, and headed over to set up my tent. It was a beautiful camping spot next to Katahdin stream, right at the base of Katahdin.

After putting up my tent I had plenty of time to kill. It may not sound exciting but the first thing I did was take a nap. I lay on my back on the picnic table provided for each campsite and proceeded to saw some zzzzzzzzz's. After that I paced back and forth for a while. I was bored. I never got into camp before 4:00 pm. I never wanted to get into camp before 4:00 pm and this was the reason why. I was bored, bored, bored! What to do. What to do. I decided to lay on my back on the picnic table, look up at the blue sky through the beautiful trees, and reminisce about my hike. Within minutes I was sawing more zzzzzzzzz's.

Finally, Juice, Mama Llama, Nature, Jeff, and Penny showed up and I visited with them. They invited me to dinner at 5:00 pm and I cooked two Lipton Noodle dinners, added a packet of salmon, and the last of my parmesan cheese. That was the last of my food. We sat around and talked as we had done many times before. I enjoyed their company. They were all nice people and interesting to talk to. Juice, Mama Llama, and Nature, had worked hard to get here. I could see the excitement and anticipation on their faces. Juice and Mama Llama had drive and discipline. They were in incredible condition. Each morning they would get up between 5:00 am and 5:30 am, have a hot breakfast, and be on their way.

While we were having dinner, we talked about the climb up Katahdin. We had been hearing about Katahdin since we started hiking the Trail. It started at 1,080' and was 5.3 miles of very challenging hiking before reaching the 5,268' summit. They knew that Doug was going to climb Katahdin with me. Juice asked me if Doug was in good enough condition to do it. I said: "He plays ping pong and climbs three flights of stairs at work instead of taking the elevator." I got five blank stares. I said: "He can do it." I knew my brother. They didn't. I believed it but just to make sure, I decided I was going to carry everything up the mountain for the two of us.

After dinner I headed back to my tent site and a few minutes later Doug showed up. It was a pure pleasure to see him. I was going to share the last part of my adventure with my brother. He looked excited to be a part of this adventure. He had come well supplied with baked chicken, peas, grapes, bananas, and all kinds of goodies. I plowed right into this second dinner and put a pretty good dent in it. There was enough left over chicken that Doug made chicken sandwiches for our lunch the next day. It was dark by the time Doug set up his tent.

We chatted before going to bed. I told Doug I would carry all of our gear in my backpack and that would free him to carry his camera and not be bothered with the weight of a pack. I could see he didn't like the idea. He started to say something and decided against it. I realized he didn't want any help. I was pleased! He carried his own pack to the top of Katahdin and back.

I had a hard time sleeping that night. I turned on my headlamp to look at my watch at least four times. The hours seemed to drag by. It was still dark when we got up the next morning. The stars were out and it was cool, breezy, and quiet. Doug had some cereal, yogurt, milk, and bananas for us for breakfast. After breakfast, we took our tents down, put them in the car, Doug parked his car in the campground parking lot, and we were on our way.

We signed a register telling when we started and there was a spot we would fill in when we returned. Nature, Juice, and Mama Llama, had signed in a half hour earlier. The first mile was gentle. We were in thick forest. We followed Katahdin Stream for a while, over bridges and past waterfalls. Doug had his camera out and was enjoying himself. He was handling the climb easily. After a mile, we were still in the forest, but it began to get steeper and rockier. When we reached tree line, we ran into some massive boulders. I was ahead of Doug and decided to tackle the boulder field alone. That way I would not distract Doug and he wouldn't distract me when we concentrated on maneuvering up, over, and around those huge boulders. The climb was very challenging. There was even re-bar in a couple of areas to help out. There were steep drop-offs to make it more interesting.

When I finished the most difficult part of the boulder field, I sat down and waited for Doug. I wasn't sure how far he was behind when I started the climb so I wasn't too concerned when he didn't show up after five minutes. I called down: "Doug?" No response. "DOUG?" Nothing.

I'm saying to myself: "Don't panic. Stay calm." "DOUG! DOUG! DOUG!" No response! Now I'm starting to panic! I take off my backpack and shoot down the area I had so laboriously climbed - re-bar and all. I can't find him and I head back up. When I get to my backpack I call:

"DOUG?"

"I'm up here."

You can imagine my relief. There was another route he had taken and he had gotten above me. As I climbed back up he snapped the photo you see on the cover.

We did more bouldering for a quarter of a mile and then found an area to have some lunch before heading up what looked to be the spine of the mountain. We were above tree line but we still had a long way to go. The views were becoming impressive. There was a mountain to our left that was still above us. There were a few small clouds, but for the most part it was sunny with a cool breeze. We had chicken sandwiches, grapes, a Nature's Way Trail Bar, and rested. Doug was doing beautifully. We hiked at a steady pace. I never had to slow down for him. We started climbing in what was called the Gateway. It was a half mile of large challenging rocks. We hiked together, finding handhold and footholds and maneuvering around and over the rocks. It took a lot of concentration and it was fun. I would look over at Doug spidering his way up a rock and see that he was totally into the moment.

After finishing the Gateway we reached the Tablelands. Everything that was living was tight to the ground. The area was covered with brown grass and compact brown shrubs. The pathway was well defined. I could see clouds forming in the distance, the breeze was picking up, but it didn't look like it was going to be a problem. Doug was taking a lot of pictures. The plant life on the Tablelands had his attention.

Half-way through the Tablelands, we met Juice, Mama Llama, Nature, Jeff, and Penny, heading down from the summit. I didn't know he was doing it but Doug was quietly taking pictures as we congratulated each other on our achievement. There were hugs and handshakes. The pictures show the excitement and genuine joy of the moment. Doug took two group pictures of Nature, Juice, Mama Llama, and me. I have never seen more teeth! Those were genuine smiles.

After saying goodbye we continued up the Tablelands. Now we were above the nearby mountain. Everything was below us. There were many lakes, ponds, and rivers in the distance. The clouds were getting darker and it was windy. A cloud was heading our way. I could see the wind currents above the Tableland by watching the cloud swirl in the air. Soon we were in its mist. It eventually drifted away and we had some visibility. I was within a quarter mile of the summit and was eagerly looking for the big Katahdin summit sign. Finally I saw people standing around and knew I was close. This was the moment I had been waiting for.

There were a few section hikers at the sign and I wanted it to be a quiet moment so I didn't tell them I was a thru-hiker. After they were finished taking their pictures I went over and touched the sign. My ultimate goal accomplished! I remember thinking: "I did it! That was a lot of work! But, Wow! That was a lot of fun!"

Doug was there to congratulate me and take pictures. He is a professional photographer and took some beauties. There is one where I'm standing behind the Katahdin sign in my yellow rain jacket that is my favorite. It shows a genuine happiness and a sense of amazement: "I really did this!?"

It was cold at the summit. The wind was whipping. I had on my warm fleece pullover and my yellow wind breaker. I had hiked every day of my thru-hike in my black shorts, red shirt, and blue baseball cap that said New Mexico on the front. I reluctantly shed the pullover and windbreaker and had my picture taken as I actually looked 99% of my hike. Then I quickly whipped those clothes back on.

A hiker reached the summit. Doug handed him his camera and got behind the sign with me. It was an excellent picture of the two of us. It was a pleasure to see that Doug was enjoying this day as much as I was. We didn't linger long. There were dark clouds in the area and it didn't look like the weather was going to be cooperating so we headed down. I was excited to have summited, but I knew getting back to the bottom of Katahdin wasn't going to be easy. I kept telling myself to stay focused. When I touched Doug's car then my thru-hike would be over.

As we headed down the Tablelands along the rocky pathway I noticed that Doug was one of those disgusting people like Slapshot, Freebird , and the Frenchman - La, who effortlessly glided over the rocks. Soon, he was two hundred yards in front of me, then four hundred, and eventually a dot in the distance. He had his camera and was doing his own thing.

This gave me a chance to be in my own little world and reflect on my journey:

"Was it a life changing event?" No.

"Did I gain any insights from this trip?" I think so. I learned I have the physical and mental capacity to endure -- and thrive. There wasn't one moment on my journey when I considered quitting. I thoroughly enjoyed myself. There were annoyances such as mosquitoes, constant rain for two straight weeks, lightning, mice, and sleeping in shelters, but I put them into perspective. The enjoyment of the Smokies, McAfee Knob, the wild ponies, the Shenandoahs, Mt. Washington, the Whites, Mahoosuc Notch, the 100 Mile Wilderness, and I can go on and on, far out-weighed any annoyances.

The Appalachian Trail Conservancy says the average time of a thru-hike is 180 days. I hiked the Trail in 148 days. I'm proud of that. It satisfies my competitive instincts.

I am adaptable. After a while, it wasn't about speed, it was about enjoyment. There were other hikers who doggedly stuck to their goal of hiking the Trail fast, even when it was physically and mentally draining them. I would read shelter journals of driven hikers who, toward the end of their thru-hike, sounded angry, exhausted, and unhappy. I slowed my hike down and enjoyed it that much more.

I am a loner. The thought of being part of a tightly knit group of four or five thru-hikers for five or six months is abhorrent to me. Many of my best memories were spent alone: The night on Cheoah Bald under the stars, sitting on McAfee Knob in the early morning, yellow eyes glowing in the dark on my night hike, following a moose to the edge of a pond and watching her forage for food, and the many nights camped alone with just the sounds of the night in Maine.

I was pleasantly surprised how much I enjoyed being around other hikers. I enjoyed visiting during breaks at shelters and at the end of the day. I made friends with a number of hikers and enjoyed their company throughout the hike. I hiked with positive people. I didn't have much time for whiners or people or groups who were loud or obnoxious.

This hike was much tougher than I anticipated. The rocks and difficult terrain defined my hike much more than I expected. Going into the hike, I thought the Trail would always allow me to stride out. That wasn't the case at all. From Pennsylvania on, there was a lot of difficult hiking on steep, rocky, pathways. In New Hampshire and Maine, much of the hiking was like a devious obstacle course. Having the hike as challenging as it was, made its completion that much more rewarding.

As I was descending Katahdin and reflecting on my hike, I concluded that I couldn't have asked for more.

The dark clouds had moved through, the winds were dying down, and it was becoming bright and sunny. I was approaching the Gateway and needed to get back into focus. Descending the gnarly rocks of the Gateway was fun and challenging. I caught up to Doug at the boulder field and we headed down together. Quite a few times in this area I slid down on my butt. Not very dignified but it worked. When we reached the place where we became separated while going up, we both took our original route down. After the boulders, it was a leisurely descent with stops at the waterfall and bridge for pictures. It was a great day and a great ending to this wonderful journey.

Have you ever taken a trip, had high expectations for it, and then have it far exceed those expectations? That would be the best way to describe my thru-hike of the Appalachian Trail. Wow! What an adventure!

DEDICATION

I would like to dedicate this book to my mother – Mary Hill. She gave my sister, brother, and me a love of adventure. She was always planning trips. She loved the outdoors. She loved to camp and walk in the woods. When she was in her late eighties, we would run eight miles each day along the bike path beside the Rio Grande River. We hardly ever missed a day. There were days in the winter when it was very cold and I would secretly be wishing we wouldn't be running that morning. I would say: "Mom, it's really cold out there. We don't have to go running if you don't want to. Do you want to run today?" Here was an 88 year old lady whose right side was paralyzed, who had lost most of her ability to speak, and was confined to a wheelchair. Her eyes sparkled with enthusiasm! "YES! YES! YES!" That's what we have to deal with. The love of adventure is in our DNA!

Wingo.

Made in the USA
Charleston, SC
25 February 2014